PRAI__

"Gargas, Ostrowski, Hughart, and Ott combine their knowledge, experiences, and insights in a book which offers practical strategies that transform the culture of a classroom. Each chapter disrupts the normal routines of classroom behaviors by engaging students through content and connections. While educators search for ways to do everything to support student learning, Teach Better has found a way to fit the educational 'puzzle pieces' together in a way that's meaningful, aligned, and seamless for the students and the educator."

—**Neil Gupta, EdD**, *director of secondary education, Worthington City Schools, ASCD board member, @drneilgupta*

"Raw! Real! Refreshing! The *Teach Better* authors declare truth bombs with honesty and vulnerability so you can do just what the title says . . . Teach Better! The vignettes, strategies, and insights are user friendly and just what we need to bring an awareness to everyday practices. This gem of a book is a welcomed gift to education!"

—**LaVonna Roth**, *creator, speaker, and lead illuminator of Ignite Your S.H.I.N.E.®, @LaVonnaRoth*

"The *Teach Better* team has written a must-read primer for anyone considering how to, frankly, teach better! As educators, we have an obligation to our students to plan, assess, evaluate, and reflect on our daily practice. How we approach pedagogy is critical to the academic, emotional, and social success of our students. This is a well-organized book with a powerful call to action to develop a *Teach Better* mindset."

—**Sheldon L. Eakins, PhD**, *director of the Leading Equity Center, @sheldoneakins*

"For educators to teach better, you'd think the approach would need to be complex. In Teach Better you're going to quickly learn that the amazing team behind the book has simplified, organized, and discussed. They've proven their methods work, and teachers are seeing the results! Rae, Tiffany, Jeff, and Chad are the minds behind this amazing book and method that is growing larger and stronger each day—and this book will undoubtedly prove to be a valuable resource across education!"

—**Adam Welcome**, *educator, speaker, author, @MrAdamWelcome*

"If you're uncomfortable with mediocrity in the classroom, this book is for you. *Teach Better* is the collective journey of four educators who share a bond. They all failed, but they all refused to allow their failure to be the end of their story. Jeff Gargas, Chad Ostrowski, Rae Hughart, and Tiffany Ott share their own personal experiences with stories that are compelling and with a vulnerability that allows them to connect with every teacher. They outline the path that allows teachers to cultivate a new 'mindset' and embrace new patterns of behavior. For new teachers who are aspiring to excellence, this book can light the way. For veteran teachers who want to reignite their flame, this book can provide the spark. But *Teach Better* is not just about educators increasing their own professional satisfaction; it's about being better for students. And that's what it's all about."

—*Danny Steele*, educator, author, and speaker

"*Teach Better* is an insightful resource filled with empowering messages for teachers at any stage in their career. It is stunning how the team weaves in deeply effective teaching strategies and curriculum based concepts in a way that feels accessible and meaningful. This collaboration is certain to impact educators with its focus on 'better' over perfect in so many areas that matter in our field. Not a surprise that this team created a relatable, useful, and impactful message in each page."

—*Sarah Johnson*, educator, speaker, author, and podcaster, @sarahsajohnson

"It's not about being perfect or about being the best. It's about becoming better. It's about mastering our craft, our calling, our labor of love for learners and learning—one optimistic step forward at a time. Backed by pithy, relatable, and engaging anecdotes from real classrooms and experiences, *Teach Better* shows us the path to continuous growth, improvement, and mastery in our practice. This is an easy but powerful read that should be required content at every school in America today."

—*Tim Cavey*, eighth-grade teacher and host of the Teachers on Fire *podcast, @TeachersOnFire*

"I've never claimed to be perfect, and I never will. Neither will you, and that's okay. In *Teach Better* the team takes us on a journey that allows us to understand that we don't need to be perfect; we just need to work every day to be better for the kids we serve. Packed with personal stories, actionable tactics, and powerful inspiration, this book will be one you reference again and again on your personal journey."

—*Thomas C. Murray*, director of innovation, Future Ready Schools, @thomascmurray

TEACH BETTER

Chad Ostrowski, Tiffany Ott, Rae Hughart, Jeff Gargas

TEACH BETTER

© 2019 by Chad Ostrowski, Tiffany Ott,
Rae Hughart, Jeff Gargas

This book is available at special discounts when purchased in
quantity for use as premiums, promotions, fundraisers, or for
educational use. For inquiries and details, contact the publisher at
books@daveburgessconsulting.com.

Published by Dave Burgess Consulting, Inc.
San Diego, CA
http://daveburgessconsulting.com

Cover Design by Genesis Kohler
Editing and Interior Design by My Writers' Connection

Library of Congress Control Number: 2019945773
Paperback ISBN: 978-1-949595-66-6
Ebook ISBN: 978-1-949595-67-3
First Printing: September 2019

DEDICATION

This book, its message, and the hours and hours of time, energy, and passion poured into it is dedicated to all of the amazing educators we are blessed to know, work with, and connect with every day. You are the reason this exists. You are the reason we do anything and everything we do. You are what *better* is truly all about.

CONTENTS

CHAPTER 1
PURSUE BETTER

"GET THE HELL OUT OF MY CLASSROOM!"

The day those uncontrolled words sprang from Chad's mouth in front of twenty-eight students is a day that changed his career—and life—forever.

———

Chad: I could feel my heart pounding in my chest and the adrenaline pumping through my veins. In that single moment, I had become something I hated, something my students never deserved, and the educator I vowed I would never be.

Sitting in the parking lot taking deep breaths to summon the courage to go into school each morning had become a sad ritual for me. I could feel myself losing faith in who I was as a teacher, and I could see it on my students' faces every day. I would stare out at the disengagement in my classroom, seeing the sad, sorry look in their eyes. Most of them wanted to focus. Most of them wanted to participate. Most of them wanted to learn. But the environment in my classroom made it almost impossible for them to do so. Those looks haunted me every day as I failed them again and again.

Something had to change.

———

Sometimes the teacher we thought we were and the priorities we thought we had get lost. Sometimes the length to which we have journeyed from our dreams shakes us to the core.

It's been said that the best thing about hitting rock bottom is that the only direction you can go is up. It was at this point in Chad's career that he had to make a decision. His only choices were to either become a better teacher or get out of the profession entirely.

Does this story feel a little familiar? Have you been there before? Are you there now? Maybe you haven't ever spoken as harshly to students sitting in your classroom as Chad did, but the despair he experienced might feel a bit more familiar to you than you would like it to feel.

It's okay.

You do not have to be sunshine and roses every moment of your career to be a phenomenal teacher. You do not have to get it right on the first try every time. You can even have meltdowns and freak-outs and moments of panic.

It's okay.

Here's the deal: Your lowest low leaves you with three options. You have a choice to make. You determine your future. You decide where your journey will lead.

Which will you choose?

Option 1: Leave education. Start over. Say ,"*Adios!*" to the career you envisioned.

Option 2: Keep on keepin' on. Dread each morning and eagerly await the end of each day.

Option 3: Make a change.

Option 3 isn't easy. It isn't fun or glamorous. It isn't going to happen without some hard work and a shift in your mindset and your actions. It might be painful. But you *can* make the change. You *can* shift your thinking. You *can* be better.

We believe in you.

The four of us have been there. We've all been to rock bottom. Whether it was Chad getting to the point of swearing at a student, Tiffany losing a job she thought was locked in for sure, Jeff failing to keep his business alive, or the start of Rae's career not going anywhere like she had dreamed it would, we have each gotten to points in our lives where we've had to make a decision.

We chose option 3. We all got there in different ways. We all made the choice for different reasons, but we all got there. We refused to give up, to give in, or to allow ourselves to continue with the unsatisfying status quo in which we'd been living. We made a choice to pursue better lives and to do it relentlessly.

Throughout this book, we're going to be sharing a lot of stories with you. We're going to share how our individual journeys came together, how our experiences led us to where we are, and the ideas and strategies we've used to get here. We're also going to share stories from some of the many amazing educators we've met along the way.

We don't share all of this because we feel we are the most awesome people who ever taught anything in the whole wide world; in fact, it's quite the opposite. Each of us is still on the journey to better. We're always tweaking, always adjusting, and always looking for ways to improve. We are constantly and continuously shifting every step of the way.

You see, a funny thing happened. Each one of us, on our individual journeys, arrived at a mindset shift that changed everything. Our twisty, turning, roundabout journeys on the paths to *better* led us to one another.

They also led us to this book—and to you. Our story is your story.

That is kind of the point of this book. It's not just to encourage you to always strive to be better. It's not just to share stories that we hope connect with you and maybe help you through some tough times. It's about so much more than that. It's about taking this journey together. It's about changing the world together. It's about being better together.

THE *TEACH BETTER* MINDSET

Teach Better is not about a specific process or practice in education. It is not about a management system or plan for communicating with home. It is not necessarily about increasing test scores or closing the achievement gap. It is a mindset, a philosophy, and a way of thinking about who we are as teachers and how we can continuously pursue *better* for ourselves and our students. It's how we push ourselves to continue growing, continue striving, and continue reaching for more.

We aren't going to lie to you. The Teach Better mindset can be challenging to embody. "Better" means being fully focused on solutions and the changes you can make instead of focusing on external factors or things that you can't change. "Better" means putting away the blame game in exchange for the solutions game. "Better" means constantly reflecting on ourselves, our strengths, our weaknesses, and our growth.

Better can be uncomfortable. Better can be scary. Better can seem futile at times. But if you commit to it fully, it can be life changing. If you always return to your relentless pursuit of better, it can change not only your life, but the lives of your students and the future of our world.

What follows in the pages of this book are stories of struggles, successes, wins, and losses. As you will quickly discover, the four of us are far from perfect. But you will also discover the shifts, the strategies, and the changes that brought us from rock bottom to a newfound love, passion, and excitement for this awesome moment in education that we live in right now. And if you let it, we believe this book can help you get there too.

––––––––

Chad: *"Get the hell out of my classroom!" The day those words escaped my mouth is the day I realized that I had lost sight of what truly mattered: my students. I was in the middle of one of the most challenging school years of my life. I was in pure survival mode every day. Every day had become a struggle. I would get sick to my stomach on Sunday nights as I tried to plan a lesson I knew was just going to blow up in my face.*

It felt like the deck was stacked against us from day one that year. I found myself in a brand-new school, with a brand-new administration, and a population of middle schoolers who had it anything but easy at home and didn't necessarily want to be there. My district had gone through a transformation, and I had moved to a new teaching position based on my experience, expertise, and interest in the STEM and problem-based learning (PBL) models.

––––––––

The school Chad taught in was in a high-needs urban district with a student population that received 100 percent free and reduced lunch. They were kids who came to school from difficult home lives. They faced more challenges before they arrived at school than a lot of people face all day. They weren't bad kids, but they were challenging.

This demographic of students wasn't new to him, though. Chad had spent his entire career in that same district. He was confident in his abilities, both in management and instruction, and he was armed with innovative strategies, new ideas, and a passion for what he was doing.

––––––––

Chad: *Something was different this time. Unlike previous years, I quickly lost confidence as I started seeing problems on a scale I had never experienced. I was facing distractions and classroom disruptions I never saw coming. I was running into roadblocks when it came to motivating students, something at which I had always been very strong. I was building relationships, but I still couldn't seem to connect with these kids like I needed to. I couldn't get them to see that I was there to help them, to lead them, and to support them along their journeys.*

I was lost. I was confused. I was ready to give up.

I couldn't decide if it was me, the school, or the students themselves, but something was not right. The bell became a release of stress and something that couldn't come fast enough. My goal became to simply "make it through" every class. My expectations for students started to drop as my management issues increased, and I started seeing problems run rampant within the four walls of my classroom. And while I wasn't the only teacher in my school struggling this way, it was a challenge I had not expected.

Chad had a choice: leave teaching and start over—abandoning the reasons he chose education as his career in the first place—or start over with *how* he taught and find a way to reach those students.

Chad: *It was time to make a change. I became more student-focused, constantly changing what I was doing in my classroom to meet their needs. I carefully observed how my students functioned in our shared space and reevaluated some of the fundamental ways I approached education. I started to create universal solutions to the problems I was seeing.*

It was by no means easy. During the summer after that worst year of my life, I spent hours and hours poring over research and making plans. When I went back to school the next year, my growth wasn't over. It was a constant process of adjusting, tweaking, modifying, and going back to the drawing board.

I knew that if I wanted to teach better, it was going to take some leg work on my part. There was no way I was going to continue on the same track. It was either get out of education or get better at what I did.

What he came up with is what we now call "The Grid Method." If you're reading this book because you've heard of it, that's awesome. If not, that's okay too. You don't need knowledge of the system for the purpose of reading this book. The important parts are that Chad's students started to achieve success at higher levels than he thought possible, his classroom management issues all but went away, and he started to enjoy—no, love—what he was doing again.

This new way of teaching was increasing his students' performances so much that other teachers in his district started to notice . . . or were being told to notice by their principals. As it turned out, he was getting stopped in the hall by other teachers wanting to know what he was doing so often that he was actually late to his own class from time to time. So he had an idea: "Maybe I should create an e-book that explains the system, and then they'll just need to ask quick follow-up questions."

A LOOK BACK AND A LEAP FORWARD

It was late, probably around 8 p.m. or so. Jeff had finished up a pretty hectic thirteen-hour day at the marketing agency he was working with, and he was tired—like, really tired. But he was also pretty excited to hear from a friend he hadn't spoken with much over the previous few years.

Jeff: I had gotten a voicemail earlier in the day from Chad, telling me he had this new way of teaching that had been working really well for his students, and some other teachers were asking about it. As I drove home, I gave him a call to talk about the e-book he wanted to create as a way of sharing his new method with his colleagues.

I ended up driving around my neighborhood block at least fifteen times or so, listening to Chad's story.

As I drove in circles, he shared with me what this new style of teaching had done for his students and for him as a teacher, and I began to get that feeling.

If you're an entrepreneur, you know the feeling I'm talking about. If you're not, I'll try to explain.

It's sort of like when you get on a roller coaster, and you're just starting to creep up that first hill. You get this little tingling in your stomach. You know it's about to be a crazy, up-and-down, spin-you-in-circles kind of ride . . . but you're super excited about it.

Now, I didn't know anything from anything when it came to education. I was a three-time college dropout. Yeah, I did pretty well in high school, but I really just knew how to play the game of school. I consider myself a fairly intelligent person, but when it came to educational theories and pedagogy, I was about as inexperienced as you can get. (I've gotten a bit better since then.)

My inexperience and lack of knowledge of the educational system didn't matter, though. I could feel it. Chad was on to something. The results he was seeing couldn't be a fluke, especially if others looked at what he was doing, thought it made sense, and saw the same results with their own students. Because this new system was helping his students and helping him as well, I didn't care what I did or did not know about the industry. I knew we had to share this with more people.

This wasn't the first time I'd had this feeling, and it certainly wasn't the first time I'd had a crazy idea. By this time in my life, I had started close to ten different business-es. Some had failed, some had done pretty well, and one had managed to support my family for the previous four years or so.

The feeling I got this time was different. I didn't know it at the time, but that car ride was about to change everything. Our lives would never be the same. And we would go on to build something bigger than we had ever dreamed possible, helping more teachers and, more importantly, more students than we could ever have hoped. And we're just getting started. We have a massive vision, built on an extremely important mission: Help teachers Teach Better and reach more students.

So I said to Chad, "Dude, we're not just writing an e-book."

———

It seems simple, like flicking a light switch, but focusing constantly on ways to improve isn't necessarily easy. We have to be okay with imperfection and failure, and we need to constantly evaluate ourselves and our ideas in the classroom.

The concept of *better* applies to all aspects of your classroom: manage-ment, planning, assessment, instruction, resources, curriculum, projects, use of tech . . . all of it! Any aspect of teaching can be changed or modified to be made better. The Teach Better mindset isn't about one single change—it's not even about *dozens* of changes. It's about constantly changing according to the needs of your students.

———

Chad: *This is the very mindset that led me out of my metaphorical "pit of despair" and into some of the best teaching I've ever done. As I began looking for causes instead of excuses, I started finding solutions in my classroom.*

Finding solutions eventually led to instructional changes. Before long, I wasn't only engaging students more than ever before, I was reaching every single learner that entered my classroom. Management issues started to be reduced, scores started to rise, and I started to love what I was doing again!

That feeling of dread that used to hit me as I pulled into the parking lot of my school was gone, and I began to feel more pride in the work I was doing every single day.

Jeff told me, "Dude, we're not just doing an e-book. You need to share this with more people. You're going to change the world."

I'm not sure I believed that last part back then, but I do now. You see, what Jeff did was teach me how to dream better. Since that day, we have worked with thousands of teachers all around the world, impacting hundreds of thousands of students that I would never have had the chance to reach had I not decided to take a leap and help others pursue better.

YOUR PURSUIT

Whether you're deciding to transform your classroom for an unforgettable unit, taking a risk and bringing more tech into a lesson, or stepping away from the classroom you love to try to change the world, the Teach Better mindset can change the way you teach, the way you look at challenges, and the way you live your life.

Every year, our students change, our resources get updated, and our educator toolbox grows (hopefully). The commitment to Teach Better is the commitment to use the tools we have, to adapt to changes that come our way, and never to be afraid to improve when things aren't going well. More importantly, it is also about the willingness to take these same steps when things are chugging along just fine. It is not enough to be reactive to the challenging circumstances in our classrooms. If we really want to Teach Better, we must embark on an endless journey of reflection, improvement, and modification.

We must always strive to reach further. It's not about being perfect or never making mistakes. It's about taking those mistakes, those challenges, those seemingly impassable roadblocks, and learning from them, making adjustments, and never giving up.

This is how *better* can become not just a word or a mindset but a way of life for educators everywhere.

Teachers are the most powerful professionals that have ever existed. The future of the world sits in our classrooms every day, and our students deserve nothing less than an unwavering and unrelenting focus on being better.

We have to believe our students can learn better, and we have to believe we can Teach Better.

That moment of reflection and realization doesn't look the same for everyone; it comes at different times and for different reasons for everyone. Chad's moment came when he considered leaving his job. Tiffany's came when she lost hers.

Tiff: *Three years into my teaching career, my husband, Cam, and I were broke, expecting our first child, behind on about a million credit card bills, and battling some health issues.*

At the time, we lived in North Carolina (both of us are originally from Ohio), and we knew that my teacher's salary could not support our growing family, let alone get us out of the hole we were in, especially since Cam was also getting ready to go back to school.

We made an incredibly difficult decision to move back home—yes, my parents' home—and try to get back on our feet. I thought that was a low moment, but I wasn't at rock bottom yet.

Once Kiya was born, I was able to get a job as a long-term substitute in Ohio that looked like it had great potential to turn into a full-time position the next year. May came around and, as it turned out, the district decided to go in a different direction.

I crashed.

I was a twenty-nine-year-old mother of a six-month-old, and I found myself asking my parents to lend me twenty dollars so I could take her to the doctor.

My husband was in school full time and working a handful of hours each week at Arby's, bringing home next to nothing.

I had no job after I let an incredible opportunity slip through my fingers because I just wasn't good enough.

I sank into despair, lower than I had ever been in my life (and I have had some pretty low moments). What good was I as a mother? What good was I as a wife? What good was I as a teacher?

The district was right to make that decision, even though it destroyed me. I simply hadn't done enough in my time as a long-term substitute to give anybody a reason to hire me full time. Yes, I taught my classes. Sure, I put together some mildly interesting experiences for my students, but was I living up to who I could be as an educator? Was I giving my students the inspiring, life-changing experiences they needed?

No.

I knew I had to up my game as an educator, but I didn't know where to even begin.

———————

Tiffany had a choice at that moment. She could look to place blame somewhere, feel sorry for herself, and potentially go on making the same mistakes, or she could take a look in the mirror, assess how she had been teaching, and make a change.

The thing is, even if we do have ideas of where to begin, or at least where we want to go, actually making those changes happen can be far more difficult than we anticipate. Our teacher preparation programs might give us countless ideas and inspiration for the kinds of classrooms we envision having, but the reality of the world sometimes makes those changes feel daunting, if not impossible.

———————

Rae: *Throughout my time in college, I had countless interactions with passionate educators regarding the implementation of best practice techniques. Up-and-coming hot topics such as standards-based grading, interdisciplinary lesson planning, mastery learning, middle school teaming, and effective classroom management were discussed constantly. There was no escaping the university's dedication to graduating forward-thinking educational leaders focused on transforming the outdated tenets of a traditional school framework.*

Nevertheless, there was a common theme. Unless an educator was able to work in an ideal environment—one with supportive administration, collaborative colleagues, engaged students, involved parents, and a proper pacing guide—the ability to enforce each progressive technique was, well, unattainable.

The unattainable theme was so pronounced, professors would often daydream of a time when the college would graduate enough passionate, driven teachers that they would one day fill a school building—and finally have the flexibility to implement all the most effective data-supported teaching techniques without limitation.

Sounds magical, right?

I was fortunate enough to accept a position teaching sixth grade in a town I had never heard of. I was over the moon to be given the opportunity to finally have my own classroom and my own students, not to mention make my own choices. So I did as any young educator does: I packed up my life in a U-Haul, adopted a senior cat from a nearby shelter so I wouldn't be alone, and started my life in a small town I called my own.

I began the first of many first days as Ms. Hughart in Room 105. The expectation at my school was for students to sit in a hard seat for forty-seven minutes, quietly take notes from lecture slides at the front of the room, follow directions from an adult, and complete homework in a timely manner.

Why would students want to dawdle? Doesn't this archaic process sound like an exhilarating way to spend eight hours of your day, 180 days a year?

Is this innovation in the making?

Seemingly unbeknownst to many professionals, most of our middle school students lived very different, unstructured lives outside of their 8 a.m. to 3 p.m.

school day. Single-parent households with adults working third shift required young kids to transition into parental roles after the school bell rang; regardless, teachers seemed to focus on spelling tests, focusing on the test grade over human development.

This was a wake-up call for me. I must be better.

We must be better.

FOCUSING YOUR PURSUIT

Jeff and Chad began their journey to Teach Better together, a partnership born from years of friendship. Tiffany's lowest moment launched her on a journey of self-reflection and growth, and Rae's refusal to give up on the "unattainable" dream of awesome learning pushed her to pursue better.

All four of us have had a moment of reflection that drove us to begin our individual pursuit of better. You have likely had that moment as well.

Take a minute before we continue to think about your moment.

Was it when you were at your lowest of lows? Was it when you suddenly had a moment of "that feeling" Jeff described when a new idea was presented to you? Was it when you saw the stark difference between your idealized vision of learning and the reality of day-to-day school life?

No matter how we got here, we can all begin to write the next chapter in our stories together. Without a doubt, we are better when we are together. We can change the world when we are together. The story of how the four of us came together is one full of unexpected connections, recognition of possibilities, and single-minded devotion to pursuing *better*.

We would love to tell you that all it takes is making a simple decision to change your outlook and perspective, but that would be a lie. It is not easy. It takes time, effort, and a lot of energy. You might have to reset and dedicate yourself to changing who you are as an educator and changing what happens in your classroom on a daily basis. You must commit to being better every single day for your students.

When you finally realize that the environment you create in your classroom is ultimately your own to control, your choices, decisions, and skills become the solutions to your problems. They are what will bring you back from rock bottom. They are what will save your career. That is what will finally allow you to be the teacher you want to be for your students.

This is our call as educators. Not to teach the students we wish we had, under the circumstances we want, but to lead the students that sit in front of us every day, using the resources we have available to us. The day Chad yelled at a student to "get the hell out" of his classroom, he realized that teaching wasn't about what he was told was best or what he wanted to do. It was about learning what his students needed, what was best for them in that moment—and in each and every moment. It was about creating a place where he could meet his students where they were and allow them to thrive.

This is the classroom we want for our students. This is the classroom we all set out to create. Most importantly, this is the classroom our students deserve.

YOU *ARE* BETTER

As an educator, we're certain you can identify a time (or two . . . or ten) when you found yourself distraught about your career and feeling as though you'd approached a fork in the road—change something or get out.

You're not alone. We've all been there.

The truth is, these moments of feeling desperate, beat down, and broken are far too common in the lives of teachers. All those moments you have in your head right now. Those moments when you felt like giving up was your only option. Those days you struggled to find anything positive to reflect on. Those mornings you dreaded walking through the doors of your building. Those nights you spent tirelessly replaying the endless wave of failures crashing down on you again and again. All of those moments . . . they could have broken you.

But they didn't break you.

You didn't quit. You didn't assume because your career was seemingly an uphill battle toward a never-ending mountaintop that it had to stay that way. You chose to find a solution anyway. You chose to change. Just like you've done by choosing to open this book. Just like you continue to do when you walk into school every day.

You see, *you* are what *Teach Better* is truly about. It's about never settling for just okay. Never allowing challenges to stop you. Never accepting "good enough" as enough.

Never stopping, never quitting, never giving up. Always striving to be better—for your students, for your family, for yourself.

You will never be perfect. But that's not the point. The point is to be better today than you were yesterday, and to be better tomorrow than you were today. That is what it means to pursue better. That's what it means to Teach Better.

CHAPTER 2
PLAN BETTER

PLANNING TO NOT PLAN

Perhaps you have heard about this strategy in business and in life. In today's fast-paced world, planning to not plan is pretty much the only way you can effectively plan. Unfortunately, a lot of people hear about it and think it means *not planning*, that they can just go with the flow, but it is quite the opposite. Planning to not plan means you have to focus on two parts, the first being the plan and the second being the "not plan."

The "Plan"

Many businesses no longer waste countless hours on business plans, because the world moves so fast. There are so many changes every day that a plan you spend twelve hours working on today will be outdated and unusable tomorrow. The strategy of not having an official business plan (that big stack of paper with hours and hours of wasted time in it that will get shoved into a desk somewhere and never looked at again) is becoming even more common as business teams shrink and become more agile.

The misconception is that these teams are simply "winging it." That is simply not true. There is a ton of planning going on; it's just not all happening on one day, and it's not being put into a hard, unchangeable document; instead, the plan is always changing, as the business is always learning. But planning happens continuously.

This couldn't be truer when it comes to you and your classroom. If you were to lay out a "business plan" for your classroom, type it all out, print it, bind it, and make it look beautiful, it would end up at the bottom of your drawer after day one. Because after day one in your classroom, that plan would no longer be the best plan for you and your students.

However, you have probably spent hours and hours and hours planning for your school year. You've reflected on the past year, adjusted your learning opportunities for your students, added new and engaging lessons, and figured out all the new supplies you'll need to be ready for pretty much anything throughout the year.

You've spent countless nights working on projects, videos, and gamification elements to make your content more engaging. You've vetted the activities you've used in past years, removed what didn't go well, reevaluated those that went okay, and used those that went really well as the standard for what your students should experience every day in your classroom.

You have planned and planned and planned, knowing all the while that, on the first day of school, you will change so many things from how you had planned them. During that first week of school, you might throw away half of what you planned as you learn more about your new students, what works for them, and what makes sense for this year. By the end of the first month of school, there's a chance your classroom and your day-to-day routines will look nothing like what you had planned.

But you still planned . . . a lot.

The "Not Plan"

You've worked so hard on planning for your year, and that is good. That is important. But the most important thing you can do is to plan to change that plan. Plan to change the way you start your day. Plan to adjust the flow of your room. Plan to swap tables for flexible seating. Plan to swap out learning activities for ones that engage your students better.

So then why have a plan at all? Why spend all that time planning?

Laying out a plan is crucial to being able to adjust on the fly. Your plan will guide you throughout the year as you make all those adjustments. Your focus should not be on only what you're going to do, because why you're doing everything you do is so much more important. As everything changes, and your plan transforms throughout the year, the "why" will guide your decisions, making sure every choice you make is done with your students in mind.

Just like an agile business that adjusts its plan day to day and minute to minute to meet its customers' most current needs, you will need to adjust your plan every day, every minute, and every second of every day to meet the needs of your students. Your plan will allow you to make those adjustments with confidence, knowing that every one of them is aligned with your why.

———————

Jeff: I've been planning to not plan for most of my adult life. Early in my career, a mentor told me, "If you focus all your attention on helping other people, you'll turn around one day and see a mountain of cash behind you."

At the time he said it, I was in sales, and he was referring to doing what's right for clients, so they stick with you and send you referrals. It is still true today, but there was an underlying message in Mike Boccia's advice, hidden to most of us in that room.

I didn't hear that message until several years later when a good friend (and another mentor) told me I was a "connector," meaning I was always looking to connect people with one another. He said, "You're a connector. You love connecting people. But you're not like a lot of other people who do it to get something for themselves. You do it because you just love helping people. And I think that's why it works, because people trust you're connecting them to other good people. That's why you have such a huge network."

That's when I realized the hidden message in Mike's earlier advice: The "mountain of cash" he mentioned was not necessarily wealth, but rather happiness and a sense of purpose and accomplishment. I made the decision then that I would never stay at a job just for the money. I would be willing to change my plans, adjust my life, and make sacrifices to stay focused on my true purpose in life: helping other people.

I've left multiple positions that paid me more than I make right now because they didn't give me a sense of purpose. I wasn't focused on helping people at those jobs, so I left.

When you leave jobs that pay well for jobs that do not pay well, it is a big adjustment, especially when you have a family to take care of. It has not always been easy; in fact, it has been hard more often than not, but I'd mentally planned for these adjustments. I knew early on that I was not going to settle for a career that just paid well. Money would never be my driving factor. I wanted to do something that helped people, that changed the world, even if only on a small scale. I wanted to leave an impact.

I had a plan. I wanted to build my own business. My original plan was to build a successful record label, because I wanted to help artists achieve success and share their passion with people. That didn't work out, so I started a promotions company, promoting concerts and music events, because I truly believe music can heal the soul like nothing else. That ended as well. Later, after learning how to build my own websites—I had to during my record label days because we had no money—I started an online marketing firm to give small businesses a more cost-effective option for their online marketing needs. That eventually ended too.

I've started somewhere around ten businesses since I was eighteen. (I honestly can't remember how many at this point.) Some of them did okay, some of them failed miserably, and one bombed so badly, I'm still paying for it. But they all had a common focus for me: helping other people chase their dreams and making a positive impact.

I knew there would be failures, reflections, and adjustments along the way, so I planned for that. I didn't know what those adjustments would be, how hard it would be at times to objectively reflect or that all those failures would lead me to working with educators all over the world, but I prepared myself mentally for the rollercoaster of a ride it would be so that I could adjust when I needed to, so I could stay focused on helping people and making that positive impact. That was, still is, and always will be my why.

———

Your classroom should be no different from Jeff's journey through entrepreneurship. You should know you're going to have failures; you're going to need to reflect (even when it's not easy to), and you're going to need to make a lot of adjustments. But as long as you have your *why*—your purpose in teaching to positively impact kids and the future of our world—you can plan for that "not plan" part of the equation.

Let's explore the plan part of the equation a bit more. Remember, we aren't telling you that you should throw out all plans and wing it—that doesn't work.

We plan and plan and plan so that when—not *if*—the need for adjustments comes, we can flexibly and quickly pivot and move in the direction that our students need. You will have a hundred different initiatives that come your way in your career. You will be challenged to change your instruction in ways that we cannot yet anticipate. You will have years and classes and students that push you to the edge of your boundaries, and you must be prepared to change everything you thought you knew.

Let's start with something concrete you can do right now. Let's change the way you plan.

RETHINKING THE TEACHER PLANNER

When we graduate from college as the proud owners of degrees that say we are allowed to teach children, we get our diplomas in the mail, official teaching certificates, and then . . .

We go hunting for the perfect teacher planner and start filling in the blanks.

Okay, maybe it doesn't exactly go in that order. Perhaps the idea of picking out a new planner each year doesn't make you excited, but for many teachers, the planner is a much-loved teaching accessory, second only to the obligatory teacher bag that lugs paperwork and lesson ideas back and forth between school and home.

Maybe you use a standard planner that your school district gives every teacher; maybe you plan with an online tool or a spare student planner the secretary gave you. Maybe you even went all out and got yourself one of those fancy Erin Cordrum planners. (You big spender, you!) Whatever your planning tool of choice, it might be time to rethink it.

What's wrong with that standard planner almost every teacher uses to plan the days, weeks, months, and year? A lot. In this chapter, we will explore the ways you have been chaining yourself to a method of planning that simply doesn't fit the world we live in today. Just like the thick business plans that can restrict companies and bind them with inflexibility, the teacher planner can limit us to a rigid fill-in-the-box, step-by-step approach to curriculum planning.

———————

Chad: During my first year as a teacher, I had a lot of preps. I was teaching regular and advanced classes at two separate grade levels. To make this even more challenging, I had a different schedule with my students from each group, depending on the day of the week. As a first-year teacher, this was a huge challenge for me. Not only was I managing multiple preps, but I also had to remember who I saw, when I saw them, and for how long.

Planning was always a struggle.

I had to get organized, so I created my own version of planning sheets that had my weekly schedule in boxes and told me who I saw when. I would use it to plan my lessons, to remind me how long I had with a given group, and to tell me when the bell was about to ring. But this document also did something else I hadn't intended: It made me plan to fill boxes rather than create learning experiences and pathways that were effective.

Every single week became a game of fill-the-boxes so I could keep my students busy. This didn't mean that I wasn't using creative lessons or engaging activities, but it did mean that I was more worried about filling the time than purposeful planning based on what my students knew, didn't know, or needed help on.

Eventually, as things settled down, I realized some of the errors I was making. I would see students respond to the day's lesson with blank stares or completely misunderstand an activity because it just didn't match up with where they were in their learning at that moment.

———

Don't worry, we aren't telling you to throw away your planners completely and never look back, but we are telling you that it is time to rethink the planner. Ask yourself, *what is the purpose of my plan book?* Is it to keep track of school events and meetings? Does it serve as a record of parent communication and notes about student needs? If so, awesome! Those are great ways to use a planner! If instead your planner serves as, well, a planner for your lessons, you should rethink how you use it.

Designing instruction that meets the needs of all your students, achieves the standards you are tasked to teach, and provides your students with a big picture of why the content is important is not something that can be accomplished by filling in the boxes of a planning book. Doing so will simply give you a day-by-day to-do list for yourself and your students, and you will miss out on opportunities for some amazing learning!

What do we do to plan *better*?

TELLING A STORY FROM A BIRD'S-EYE VIEW

Back away from the planner. Close the Google document where you started to write your plans. Kick back in your chair and engage one of your most valuable tools in planning: your imagination!

Before we launch into standards and targets and pacing (Don't worry—we are getting there!), let's talk about the step that should come first if you really want to build the kinds of units that will wow your students, pull them deep into the learning, and imprint the concepts in their minds. Too often we skip this step and are left with daily and weekly plans that can feel uninspired to us and uninteresting to students. Not a great combo.

Consider first the story you are trying to tell with the content. The order in which we introduce material should not come from the textbook or from the order of standards listed on the state Department of Education webpage. It should come from an understanding of what the purpose of the standards are and what meaning they have together.

Tiff: My first few years of teaching, I worked at a middle school in North Carolina teaching science. What fun it was! We got to play around with lab equipment, explore how the world (and universe) worked, and dive deeply into our wonderings.

I was hired in January for an unexpected opening the school had and so came into a classroom that already had routines and procedures in place as well as the semester of content mapped out. I was endlessly grateful for this, as there had been about one week from when I was hired to when I moved out of state, set up shop in my sister's friend's house, and took over the classroom.

When the next year rolled around, I knew I wanted to mix it up a bit and veer off of the preestablished order of daily lessons. I still had to follow the district pacing calendar, of course, but I took the time to explore the topics for each unit and let my imagination run wild.

What were the connecting threads between the scientific method, plate tectonics, and volcanism? How did those ideas link to studying the solar system or to ecology? I discovered a story of interwoven phenomena that link together in fascinating—and sometimes unexpected—ways.

Rather than starting the year with lessons about what the scientific method is, we discovered a natural phenomenon as real scientists, exploring, testing, revising, and concluding. What started as an experiment to determine why Diet Cokes float and Cokes sink led to student discovery of density, which became the connecting thread through all the content we studied during the year.

Plate tectonics became an exploration of how density directly shaped the face of the Earth. This led to wonderings about how it might impact other worlds in the solar system. Density connected again to the content as we considered how inter-woven groups of living organisms interact with each other.

The story we told was one of how a tiny, easily overlooked phenomenon shapes the world in massive and tiny ways. Everything from bacteria to the universe is connected in this story of mass, volume, and whether something floats or not.

———————

Take the time to let your imagination play with the content you are tasked to teach. Sketch out ideas on a napkin at the local diner. Put seemingly uncon-nected ideas on separate Post-It notes spread all over your table, and arrange, rearrange, and shift again until the story starts to become clear. Record yourself talking about the standards and how they might connect in a stream-of-con-sciousness babble, then go back and listen to find the nuggets of insight you create.

Just like a good book that you struggle to put down late at night when you know you should be sleeping, the content that we share with students should pull them into the stories of your subject. Only once you have played with these ideas and discovered the plot of the learning should you then move forward and begin designing the learning experiences that students will take on to dis-cover this story themselves.

GETTING DOWN TO BUSINESS

Now that you know the purpose of the learning and the story that weaves through and among the standards, it is time to start breaking down those stan-dards into actual learning opportunities. And it's time to do it without relying on your textbook or curriculum materials.

Don't misinterpret what we are saying—textbooks can be excellent tools and invaluable resources, and the need for high-quality curricular materials cannot be disregarded, but you can't rely on them too heavily. Deeply examining and breaking down the standards into leveled learning targets is hard. It is not a fast process, and it will likely leave you feeling like your brain is fried. But it is a critical part of designing exceptional learning experiences and is well worth the time and effort you put in.

How do you do it? One of our favorite ways is to think of our standards in the framework of depth of knowledge (DOK).

Dr. Norman Webb developed DOK as a framework through which to under-stand the complexity of thinking that students must use during a learning opportunity. There are books, articles, webinars, and professional development workshops all about DOK, and they are widely available. We won't go into huge detail here about all of that, but we do want to give you a sense of what DOK is because it is a fundamental part of how each of us plans instruction for our students.

———

Tiff: I admit, I had no idea what DOK was before I met Chad. When I was in college, we talked mostly about Bloom's Taxonomy of Learning, and although there are some similarities between Bloom's and DOK, there are enough differences that learning about DOK rocked my thinking about student thought significantly.

I was sitting on the floor of my living room on a Google Hangout with Chad as he taught me about the structure for mastery learning that he had created. As we talked, he mentioned DOK, and I had to stop him to ask for clarification on an example of DOK. I remember Chad explaining the different levels of DOK to me by using game shows as a metaphor. (We actually can't give Chad credit for this brilliant explanation! Erik Francis, an awesome educator and consultant from Arizona, gets that credit!)

Here is how he broke it down:

———

DOK 1

Is all about recall and reproduction. Similar to the "Remember" and "Understand" levels of Bloom's, this level requires little complex thought beyond memorization and understanding. Think of this level as *Jeopardy*. Contestants have to pull information from their brains to answer questions on Jeopardy, and students have to pull information from their brains to answer DOK 1 questions.

DOK 2

Takes the knowledge from a DOK 1–type question and asks students to apply it. Game show analogy for this? *Top Chef! Top Chef* contestants don't just rattle off a bunch of information about proper

NOT FAMILIAR WITH WEBB'S DEPTH OF KNOWLEDGE?

Check out TeachBetter.com/ BookResources for a link to a free course about DOK.

cooking temperature for chicken or the ingredients in a cake; they instead apply this information and put the concepts into action. A student might know what a simile is and what a metaphor is (DOK 1), but applying this knowledge to compare and contrast the two or explain why an author uses one over the other kicks it up to DOK 2.

DOK 3

Defend your answer. Prove your ideas. Support your reasons. These are all DOK 3 tasks! Beyond application of information in isolated instances, DOK 3 takes things to the next level. Think about the long-running show *Survivor*. Collaboration, explanation of ideas, and attempts to sway others to your opinion are key components of success on this show, and they are key components of success on a DOK 3 task.

DOK 4

What do you do when you have learned about a concept, understood how it compares with other ideas, and been able to defend an answer about that concept with evidence? You take that knowledge and apply it in a new context, extending the ideas in new directions and with new insight. That is DOK 4. Think about the show *Shark Tank*. At the core of the show is the creation of new products or services designed to meet a need. Contestants justify an innovation to a panel of judges, supporting the need for their invention with arguments built on a solid understanding of concepts and facts applied in a new invention.

Tiff: Whew! Thank goodness I had Chad Ostrowski (and he had Erik Francis) to help me make sense of this DOK stuff. Let me tell you, once I began actually applying these ideas and breaking down my standards into learning targets based on DOK, I started thinking about the content I was teaching in a completely different way.

Was it tedious? Yes. Time consuming? You bet. Worth it? Absolutely.

BREAKING DOWN STANDARDS

Now is a great time to go grab a notebook and pencil or create a new document on your computer. At the very least, think of a standard you teach and spend a few minutes mentally exploring the different levels of complexity that standard contains.

Let's look at some examples from a few different content areas:

Example 1: Social Studies Content

TOPIC	American Revolution	CONTENT STANDARD	Explain why the American colonists united to fight for independence from Great Britain and form a new nation.	GRADE	7
DOK 1 LEARNING TARGET		I can identify important events, individuals, and ideas from the American Revolution era.			
DOK 2 LEARNING TARGET		I can interpret an author's meaning and purpose in writing.			
		I can compare Thomas Paine's and John Locke's ideas about the American Revolution.			
DOK 3 LEARNING TARGET		I can draw conclusions about the events of the American Revolution.			
		I can assess and interpret the meaning of Thomas Paine's message.			
DOK 4 LEARNING TARGET		I can use my understanding of the American Revolution to recommend policy strategies in the Middle East.			

Each level builds on the previous and relies on what has come before, leading to increasingly complex thinking and exploration of ideas. Most of what we tend to focus on in class are DOK 1 and 2 tasks. News flash: Most standards aren't written on DOK 1! Only a few are asking students to complete DOK 2 tasks, and most of them are actually written at DOK 3.

Schools tend to test our students on facts and concepts. We lean on memorization and regurgitation as the backbone of our daily routines. But we are missing depth if we don't take the time to consider how that information can push into DOKs 3 and 4!

Let's look at another example of a science standard broken down into DOK levels:

Example 2: Science Content

TOPIC	Cycles of the Earth and Moon	CONTENT STANDARD	The relative patterns of motion and positions of the Earth, moon, and sun cause solar and lunar eclipses, tides, and phases of the moon.	GRADE	7
DOK 1 **LEARNING TARGET**		I can define and explain how the moon's change in position around Earth leads to changes in its appearance (phases) as well as lunar and solar eclipses.			
DOK 2 **LEARNING TARGET**		I can apply and demonstrate knowledge of how the moon's change in position and phases around Earth lead to high and low as well as neap and spring tides on Earth due to its gravitational pull.			
DOK 3 **LEARNING TARGET**		I can compare and contrast the patterns of the moon's position and phases with its visual appearance, eclipses, and tides.			
DOK 4 **LEARNING TARGET**		I can construct and design a model or demonstration (physical or digital) of how the moon's position compared to Earth creates the phenomena of phases, eclipses, and tides.			

Here is why you must move beyond your plan book and your textbook. Exploring how a standard changes as you move through the DOK levels helps you see the big picture of the goal of the standard. It helps tell the story of the content and shows you how it connects to other learning, other subjects, and the greater world. Even if you don't use all of the ideas you came up with for DOK 4 learning targets, exploring what those ideas look like helps you understand what you are tasked to teach. It is well worth the effort to do this exploration yourself!

Let's draw a parallel between the work we are asking you to do here by breaking down standards and the work we ask our students to do in the classroom.

Tiff: *If any of you reading are parents of adolescents, are middle or secondary teachers, or have any recollection of what your own experiences as a teen were like, perhaps you can relate to some of the following story.*

Me: "I don't care about the answer. I care about the thinking."

Cue sighs, eye rolls, and persistent arguments from most of the class.

Student: "But I got the answer right! Why wouldn't I get credit if the answer is correct?"

Me: "I don't care about the answer. I care about the thinking. Explain your answer to me."

Student: "What do you mean? $x^3 \cdot x^4 = x^7$ *That is the rule—you add the exponents!"*

Me: "Yes, but why?"

Student: "Because that is the rule!"

Me: "The rule is not enough. Get to the why of the rule and then we can move on."

Cue more eye rolls and sighs. But when we persist and they discover themselves the reason for why the exponent rules work, that learning is going to stick so much more than if I were to simply allow them to use the rules without deeper thought.

If I hadn't taken the time to really break the standard down beyond simplifying exponents, I would not have designed a learning experience that asked students to justify, prove, and discover patterns in the ways exponents work.

Students had a richer thinking experience (even if they were initially frustrated) because of my willingness to take the time and break the standard down.

You should repeat this process with each standard you are tasked to teach. Discover the deeper complexity in everything you teach. Use your colleagues as additional brains to help think through the content, but don't rely exclusively on the thinking of others. Just as Tiffany's students discovered greater meaning by discovering the exponent rules themselves, you will discover greater meaning in the standards by discovering their complexity yourself.

One other note on these standards: remember the story you imagined earlier in this chapter? The interwoven, connected, exciting story you are trying to help your students explore? As you work through the process of breaking down standards, be open to how the story you discovered in the previous step might change once you more completely understand the standards you are trying to teach. Remember, the Teach Better mindset is about flexibility, reflection, and adjustments, and planning better is no exception.

RETHINK YOUR PLANNING.
RETHINK YOUR PACING.

Now that you have discovered the story you want to tell with the content and deeply examined your content standards—dissecting them into increasing levels of complexity—you can start to think about how these pieces will come together into a unit. We challenge you to continue to sever the relationship with your teacher planner and start to think about planning in a totally different way. Rather than planning out what you will do Monday through Friday each week, throw out that calendar and think of what steps your students will take on the journey toward understanding.

It is time to rethink the way you pace your classroom.

We are so well trained to think of learning as a sequence of daily lessons that it is difficult to move beyond that. Let's face it, our experiences as students ourselves is almost surely from a world in which the teacher decided what happened Monday, Tuesday, Wednesday, Thursday, and Friday. When you came into class each day, you waited for your teacher to tell you what you were doing and then you did it.

Perhaps you function in the same way as a teacher. You plan out your daily lessons in your plan book and know what is happening Monday through Friday in your class.

Monday: Hook students into the new unit on ecology with a game and introduce basic vocabulary for the unit.

Tuesday: Review vocabulary and watch a video on ecosystems around the world while students take notes.

Wednesday: Explore different kinds of symbiosis with an interactive simulation.

Thursday: Review game for the weekly quiz tomorrow.

Friday: Crossword puzzle to review followed by a quiz.

Here is the catch, though: Are your students ready to understand the simulation you have planned for Wednesday if most of them are still struggling to identify a producer and a consumer? Is the video on different ecosystems effective if a student still doesn't know what an ecosystem is and why they are learning about them? And what about that Friday quiz? You know when you hand it out that some of the students just aren't ready for it, will struggle, and will likely earn a low score. Or perhaps some of your students could have aced it on Tuesday!

The problem with all of this is that you are dictating a pacing timeline for your students, moving all of them through the content at the same time.

Don't we know by now that one-size-fits-all clothing should actually be called one-size-fits-some?

Isn't it time to recognize that one-size-fits-all pacing is actually one-size-fits-some?

———

Rae: Pacing is difficult. I remember my first year teaching, striving to master the endless obligations required to be a strong educator—engaging learning opportunities, rigorous content, communication with parents, building relationships with students, assessing understanding, classroom management, evaluation cycles—the list goes on and on; however, in the midst of all the juggling, trying to master the right "pacing" for all thirty-four students seemed like a comical joke played on young educators.

I chose to pace to the middle. If the majority of my classroom understood the content, and I had gone over what I deemed to be the appropriate content in what I felt was the appropriate amount of time, it was time to move on. With this method, I felt as though I was reaching most of my students most of the time. And that's all an educator could ask for, right?

Oh, how wrong I was.

Student-paced mastery learning actually works using the Grid Method. I learned it from Chad himself. In front of a packed audience, he started off his session discussing his beautiful family and a fun story about how babies learn to walk. He then posed a very blunt question to all of us in the room:

"On average, how many students do you reach in your classroom?"

As you can imagine, the room was silent as we all pondered the question. Thankfully, it was multiple choice, so we only had a few options to choose from.

  A. None
  B. Some of them
  C. Most of them
  D. All of them

I thought to myself: C. Most of them, *and I have to tell you, I felt pretty good about my response. Most is pretty great, right? I am an awesome teacher, making a difference in most of my students' academic lives. Come on, that's pretty awesome! I mean, I am no Superman, but I'm not too far off from getting my own shiny cape!*

Let's be realistic here—if you are reaching most of your students, there are probably a couple kids on the enrichment end that you may not be challenging enough, and a couple on the low end whose gaps in understanding you haven't been able to fill in enough to catch them up to grade level. But eighty percent is pretty good! Right?

Wrong.

If we plan our units day by day, designing lessons that move students along a predetermined path at a predetermined time, we are, at best, only reaching most of our students. Sure, we have intervention programs for the students that struggle most and maybe the really advanced students get the chance to go to an enrichment class sometimes, but the day-to-day, minute-by-minute teaching we do just doesn't cut it for all students.

Instead, what if you rearranged the learning experiences your students have to move at the pace of the individual student? Imagine each child moving through content at his or her own pace, showing understanding of the material before moving on so gaps in understanding simply cease to exist. Imagine extending students' thinking and moving to higher levels of complexity when they are able to, not when there are only fifteen or twenty minutes left in class every once in a while in which they can work on logic puzzles.

A STUDENT-PACED MODEL

If only it were that simple. We aren't going to lie to you; moving to a self-paced learning environment is not a walk in the park. It will challenge you, push you, and make your head spin sometimes. To be honest, we could write an entire book about the student pacing model we cover here. But it would be cruel to tell you how awesome student pacing can be and expound on the transformative impact it can have on your students and yourself as an educator without then giving you at least a quick overview of how you can plan pacing that meets your students' needs and timelines rather than your own.

The good news? If you have done the work of breaking down those standards into DOK levels 1

WHAT'S THE GRID METHOD?

We talk a lot about The Grid Method in this book, but this is not a book about The Grid Method. Check out teachbetter. com/bookresources for additional information, like links to a free course, sample grids, and more.

through 4, you have already taken some huge steps on your journey to self-pacing. Let's explore how these DOK targets can become the backbone of something we call the Grid Method.

Here is how it works (the CliffsNotes version):

Disclaimer: We do not advise running off and trying to create Grids to use in your class right now. Our brief explanation here will not give you all the context you need to fully and successfully implement student-paced learning in your classroom.

Step 1

Identify the standards for a unit you teach. Make sure you take the time to determine the story you want students to discover about these standards. This is the part where you get to imagine and dream big!

Step 2

Break down your standards into learning targets leveled by DOK complexity. If you have been working through these steps as you read this chapter, you are already one third of the way there!

Step 3

Decide what you need your students to do to demonstrate understanding of each learning target you created. We will call these your "Mastery Questions."

Step 4

Build learning experiences for your students that will help them answer these questions. This doesn't have to mean reinventing the wheel! Use resources you already have and love, the ones that you know have a track record of helping students learn.

Step 5

Put it all into a Grid, which will provide a learning path that students will take through the increasingly complex learning targets you created in step 2.

Step 6

As students move through this Grid, require them to show mastery of a learning opportunity before moving on to the next.

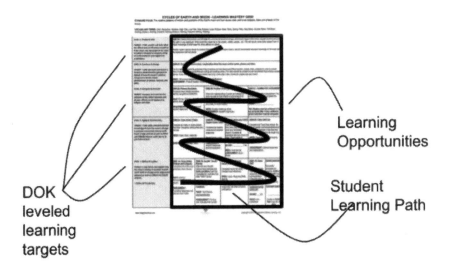

DOK leveled learning targets

Learning Opportunities

Student Learning Path

Yes, this approach means your students will all be working on different things at different times.

Yes, this means that you must have your unit planned out before you begin.

Yes, this means that you may have to rethink the structure of your days and weeks.

But consider this: Being open to trying this approach could mean that students in your class will be learning content when they are ready, moving through understanding at the pace that works for them. You will be reaching all your students with the content they need when they are ready for it at the moment they need it.

PROCEED WITH CAUTION

Self-paced learning can be an awesome tool. It can free you from the shackles of pacing that doesn't meet your students' needs. It has a proven track record of incredible student achievement if implemented well. It is, frankly, awesome. Anytime you can make your classroom more student-centered and meet the needs of more students, you're going to increase achievement for your learners!

But it doesn't always go the way we want it to. Sometimes self-paced learning can go very wrong. Regardless of how much positive data and research exist for learning that allows students to master material (And there is *a lot*—see Google), even the best pedagogy can be destroyed by improper or poor implementation.

We want to arm you with the knowledge of the biggest pitfalls that happen when teachers try to implement self-paced learning so that you enter into this bold new adventure prepared.

1. Self-paced learning is not self-taught.

We work with a lot of teachers and districts to help them implement mastery and student-paced learning, and we run into a common misconception over and over again. Just because a student is learning at their own pace with increased independence and control over their learning path does NOT mean that they are completely in charge of their learning. Providing students with access to content and curriculum at the pace they need does not mean they will know how to understand, interpret, and use this information.

When educators first hear about self-paced learning, many of them think that because students are accessing content or curriculum at their own pace that they are also supposed to learn on their own. You, the teacher, are the master architect behind these learning experiences. You, the teacher, are the guide that can lead your students to explore the content effectively.

2. Self-paced learning should mean more teaching, not less.

One of the primary concerns we hear from teachers honestly kind of baffles us. When we share ideas of self-paced learning at workshops, conferences, and in online forums, we often hear, "When do I actually teach?"

It's time to rethink the definition of teacher. You are not a content deliverer. It is absolutely no longer your job to tell students information, because they don't need that anymore.

Think about this. Let's say a science teacher's job is to teach biology. If that teacher views his or her job as one of content delivery, the teacher is no better than YouTube. Yes, a website that has existed for a mere fourteen years (as of 2019) has replaced us as content experts.

So, what are we? What do we do? If we are no longer in charge of content delivery, what is it that we do exactly?

Our job is now to help students find, judge, understand, and interpret content. Our job is to show them how to use the content. For a very long time, many educators have tended to focus on lower levels of questioning built on rote memorization and knowing of facts. This is understandable because, as the experts in our subject, we had to impart content into our students' minds.

Ready for a real challenge to your thinking?

There might not be a need for your students to know the difference between a producer and a consumer in their future lives. They probably do not need to know how to do triple-digit multiplication using the traditional algorithm— we all have calculators on our phones. Memorizing the sequence of dates and events in the American Revolution is probably not something that will help our students in their adult lives.

All of these tidbits of information can be searched on Google in less than a second. If they can type a question into a search engine, they can get an answer faster than you can teach it to them.

So what if we curate content and then allow our students to explore it and be inspired? We can challenge them to think in new ways and apply the content to problems and challenges faced in the present day and those of the future. What if we teach them how to self-regulate and discover an internal drive for understanding and growth? We don't do this by talking at them in what we have long considered "teaching." That's not what teaching is anymore.

When do you teach?

In a self-paced classroom environment, you teach every second of every day. You teach in the two-minute conversation with a student to clarify a misunderstanding. You teach in the way you observe student behavior and mood and respond appropriately. You teach in the ways you reflect and adjust the learning path you design for students to follow. You teach in the curation of resources you do and the experiences you build that allow students to explore these resources. You teach. All. The. Time.

3. Self-paced learning doesn't always start where you think it will.

If you have children or have been around children for any length of time since 2016, chances are you have heard of the movie *Moana*. If you haven't, you should definitely go watch it. Tiffany cried like a baby multiple times in the movie and still tries to get her kids to watch it every chance she has, and Jeff can't say "you're welcome" without singing the song of the same name.

What does this have to do with teaching?

One of characters in the movie is Maui, a shape-shifter, demigod of the wind and sea, and hero of men. He also happens to be a villain-turned-world-saver. At one point in the movie, he teaches Moana, the heroine of the story, how to be a way finder (an expert sailor). In teaching her, he says,

"IT'S CALLED WAYFINDING, PRINCESS. IT'S NOT JUST SAILS AND KNOTS, IT'S SEEING WHERE YOU'RE GOING IN YOUR MIND. KNOWING WHERE YOU ARE BY KNOWING WHERE YOU'VE BEEN."

Wow—the depth in that statement! We could go on a philosophical tangent here that explores the deeper meaning of that sentence and applicability to our lives, but we will settle for seeing its meaning for us as educators. Knowing where our students are by knowing where they have been is not optional for us. Understanding what our students understand is not something we can figure out as we go; it is something we must know as we begin to plan better.

We must pre-assess. We must discover what our students know. Failing to do so is like trying to navigate the ocean with no compass, no GPS, and no understanding of how the stars can tell us where we are.

In short, failing to know where our students are and what they understand is one of the most foolish unit-planning errors we can make. It is also one of the easiest to correct.

Rae: *My teacher training program had a significant focus on evaluating students' background knowledge through pre-assessment, then, most importantly, using this assessment information to inform the pacing of each unit.*

*I recently spent hours planning a volume unit for my accelerated math class. It was epic! I tied in a real-world theme and scaffolded information to ensure students would feel confident with the content. Feeling a bit rushed, I chose to **skip the pre-test** and dive right into student learning. Within the first thirty minutes of class, students were already voicing their confidence on the test.*

What? I thought, astonished. This was supposed to last me all week!

Little did I know, my students already carried so much background knowledge on this topic, they didn't need much time to master the information. They were ready to challenge themselves with enrichment.

Take the time to administer a pre-test or identify your students' existing knowledge on a subject so you can effectively plan learning experiences that meet their needs. Only then can you know where the pacing of learning can start for each individual student.

We won't sugarcoat it; pacing is difficult. But it's only difficult because the ones who know the pace necessary for mastery are not the ones in the driver's seat. It is the students who have the most information about where they need to go and how fast they need to go to get there, not the teacher. Hand them the keys. Print a detailed map. Buckle up beside them. Hit the gas. Zoom!

PLAN TO PERSONALIZE

We've explored the big-picture story we try to help our students see. We understand our standards through the lens of DOK. We have begun to explore the ways changing the pacing of learning to match student needs can take education to the next level. Now what?

So much of what we have talked about with planning is how you can move your plans to a student-focused and student-centered learning experience. Honoring their prior knowledge and the pacing they need is no longer optional in education. Helping them see the greater purpose through the story we pull them into must be done if we want to help grow connected, world-changing humans.

Let's take a few minutes to acknowledge that. Every day in our classrooms, we are crafting the future leaders of our world. We are actively sculpting the generation that will have to grapple with increasing world population, the effects of climate change, diminishing resources, and increasing challenges from a world bound by complex webs of geographical, political, and economic threads.

What do we need these children to become?

They should be advocates for what is right in the world. They must be able to communicate and collaborate with people who are different from them. They must be reflective and constantly open to growth, because the world around them is growing and changing in ways we cannot possibly predict.

What we don't need? Humans who blindly follow the rules and schedules imposed upon them and sit quietly, following directions.

We need rebels. Challengers. Innovators. Boundary pushers. We need people who speak up for their needs and help craft the world around them. And we need to start building that right now in our classrooms. How do we do that?

We start by asking and listening.

Ask your students what they should be learning and how. Ask them to help craft the learning experiences they want. Trust them to think deeply about the challenges of modern education and help you design the kind of learning they need. These kids are not I. They know that the world is different for them than it was for us. They know there is a push and pull among regulations, standards, testing, and protocols as well as innovation, individualization, meaning, and purpose.

As we strive to do our best to reach all of our learners, connecting individually with each student, and designing dynamic lesson plans to ensure that students meet mastery on content, we often forget to stop, listen, and ask questions to the most important people in our classroom—our students.

Then why don't we do this?

The truth is, most educators are scared. Scared of what they might find out if they stopped to ask their students how their instruction is going. Many feel this question to a student welcomes criticism (and it might). They might tell you they hate how you teach. They might tell you that class is boring and useless to them. As they pour out their hearts to you about everything they feel you're doing wrong, you have one single job: **Just listen**.

Listen to your students' ideas. Listen to your students' struggles. Listen to your students' explanations. Listen to your students.

Tiff: *I admit, I am confused. In every district I have taught (five and counting) most teachers have a predictable and frightening reaction to the concept of student surveys and student evaluation. In one, teachers raged with fire and fury at the concept of seeking student feedback midyear rather than in the traditional May survey window. Frightened about the impact of these student feedback surveys on their own evaluation and, potentially, the impact these surveys might have on their careers, they responded with a whole slew of reasons why it was a terrible idea:*

"Students don't know enough to provide valuable feedback on quality teaching."

"What if they rate me lower because they don't like science (or math, or history, or . . .)?"

"Students aren't reliable."

"I don't trust administration to not use this against me."

"I am the expert in education, not my students."

Yes, every one of those sentences passed the lips of my colleagues. Is it any surprise that so many students don't trust us to have their best interest and their happiness in mind? Is it any wonder that there is an underlying current of frustration, disinterest, and disillusionment in the complex connection between student and teacher?

We need to get over it. Some of our students will reply to these surveys or requests for feedback with rage. Here are some recent responses to a survey I gave my students—actively seeking their feedback so that I could improve:

In response to "What do you wish was different about this course?" a student said the following:

"I wish that we learned stuff that was actually relevant to life because I'm not going to graph an inequality in the middle of the summer while I'm swimming."

(Ouch. Math teacher pain right here.)

In response to "What do you want to stay the same about this course?" a student said the following:

"Nothing. I dread coming to this class and I don't think that's gonna change."

But along with this negativity and distrust came the following responses:

"I wish we did activities outside of class as a class to create a stronger bond with the class as a whole."

"I wish that we didn't get as much homework and I also don't like the videos we have to watch."

————

When you seek feedback, you sometimes get burned, but you also sometimes get nuggets of insight from your students that you would not otherwise have seen. Tiffany's students wanted relevance, purpose in what they did, and a greater sense of community. They also didn't want to learn about inequalities, but since it was a freshman math class, that really wasn't an option. But could she find some way to make those inequalities matter more to students? She wasn't sure how, but you better believe she took that feedback and made adjustments to her course.

Not everything your students ask of you will be doable, and it's okay to take each suggestion or critique with a grain of salt; nevertheless, the relationships you build with your students, the respect you build with your students, and the reflection you have with your students are invaluable to truly ensure you reach as many students as possible.

Plan to Change Who You Are as a Teacher

We have thrown a whole bunch of ideas and a ton of information at you in the last few pages. We have asked you do to a lot in terms of rethinking your instruction, your planning, your pacing, and the very fundamental assumptions you have about yourself as an educator. Those challenges to your thinking are not going to end here, and by the time you finish this book, you may feel like you have a brain made of Jell-O. You may feel overwhelmed or frustrated. You may feel like the goals are too far off for you to reach and that you just can't attain the kind of teaching we're saying you must do.

Take a step back right now and prepare yourself for the journey ahead.

You became a teacher because you wanted to make an impact. You wanted to positively change the lives of your students. Maybe you feel like you've done this pretty well so far, maybe you don't. Maybe you feel like you're struggling every day to remember why you started. Wherever you are in your journey, you know where to start: with one step and one decision.

You will make plans for how you will change and grow. You will implement systems and routines that will help you plan better, grade better, assess better, and start better. And they probably won't work out exactly how you have planned.

Don't beat yourself up if that original plan you had doesn't work or if the fifteen other plans you've come up with don't work so well either. Reflect, adjust, and remember the original purpose of your plan: to impact students' lives.

STORIES FROM THE TEACH BETTER COMMUNITY

> PAM ERICKSON (@PERICKSON22)
Fourth Grade Teacher, Minnesota

Have you ever taught a lesson you planned out really well, and during that twenty-five minutes of talking, you were addressing behaviors the whole time? A part of the class has been doodling, another part barely awake, and another part has decided there are things way more important to talk to their friends about than listening to what information you have to give them. The million-dollar question is HOW DO I ENGAGE THESE KIDS?

At a conference last year, I signed up for a class called Teach Better, and honestly I didn't even read the description but thought to myself *I would like to teach better, so let's see what it is about*. Little did I know that class and Rae

Hughart would change my classroom and how I teach drastically. I learned about The Grid Method and how to ensure mastery learning as the students progressed through the DOK levels, which was amazing, but even further, Rae showed me how she presented her lessons and learning activities all in one place so the students could move through them at their own pace.

Basically, it was a flipped classroom IN the classroom, so I could help them at any point they needed and have meaningful one-on-one or small group lessons at the level where the students were while the rest of the class moved forward. There would be no more dragging kids along while others were bored because they already knew the content. As soon as I got back from the conference, my grade partner and I went to work, and it was the best decision we have ever made for our students.

There are times when everyone is working, and I back into a corner of my classroom and take it all in, as every single student is engaged in their own learning at their own pace and their own level. Not only that, but I had one particular student who struggled in math take her Chromebook home to work because she so desperately wanted to get to the enrichment activity before the unit was done. While working at home, her mom taught her a strategy I had never thought of, so I asked her to make a video that we added to our grid to help others. I watched her confidence soar in a subject that typically had made her feel like a failure.

I will be forever grateful to the amazing Teach Better Team for their support in my journey that has made me "Teach Better" for my students.

CHAPTER 3
CONNECT BETTER

Even though we just spent a whole chapter talking about planning, standards, and pacing, we do not teach to follow a pacing guide, teach math facts, or explain the order of planets in the solar system. Dates of ancient wars and names of generals are not the goals. We strive not for parrots who can mimic what we have told them, but for thinkers, dreamers, and doers. The problem is, we often find ourselves in situations that run contrary to all the reasons we started teaching.

The grade-level standards, testing, assemblies, and endless to-do lists of teaching rapidly crowd out the most critical aspects of what we believe about the job we have chosen to make our careers, and it can be hard to keep our eyes on the prize we set out to find. We end up wandering through the textbook pages and worksheets and common assessments only to reach a point where we ask ourselves, *What am I doing here?*

Tiff: *"Hi there, Amber."*

"Hi, Mrs. Ott. Can I come into your room again this morning?"

"Sure, Amber. Come on in."

Amber was a regular fixture in my sixth-grade classroom that year. Every time she saw me walking into the building, she would ask if she could come hang out with me before school. Sometimes she would bring a friend; other times she would come alone. Sometimes she would chat my ear off as I was trying to get last-minute things ready for the day; other times she would sit quietly, reading a book.

Amber had a bit of a reputation as an attention seeker in the school. She was an emotionally charged kid who went from extremes of happy exuberance to sad, silent tears rolling down her cheeks. She was eleven years old, perched right at the cusp of puberty, struggling to identify who she was and where she fit in this great big world that she was just beginning to make sense of.

Other teachers would tell me that I shouldn't have her in my room every morning, that it was just encouraging her to seek out even more attention. They said that it made me too available to my students and that I would run out of time to do the things I needed to do to teach. They told me that being so emotionally invested in my students was going to burn me out fast.

I admit, I didn't listen to them.

———

Tiffany ignored the advice some of her colleagues gave her. They were well-meaning, for sure, but they completely missed the boat on a major piece of our work as educators. What Tiffany discovered early in her career was that these connections were the key to keeping her invested in and interested in her job. It wasn't just about being there for a struggling student; the moments she gave to her students grounded her in what she loved so much about her job.

Connections matter. Most educators we talk to recognize the importance of positive relationships with students; in fact, we have never come across a teacher who adamantly believes that students couldn't benefit from a connection formed with their teacher. But connections go beyond the conversations we have with our individual students. They also extend to the relationships we might build with the teacher down the hall. They can even reach far across the globe, building a network of teachers united in a vision of better learning experiences for their students.

Connections are the keys that bind our students to this world, to learning, and to the futures that they will build. Unfortunately, it is often those connections that are the first to go when teachers face an increasingly stressful, demanding job.

SEEING THROUGH THE STRESS

Up to your ears in paperwork? Grades due next week? Extra meeting on Thursday about a student who may be retained? Fifteen more standards to cram in before the common assessment next month?

When we are struggling in our jobs, it is easy to become jaded and shut down. Each one of us has been there. Each one of us has come to a point where we were surviving, eking out an existence day to day and barely making it to that final bell.

It can feel like every time we turn the corner in the hallway or walk in the front door in the morning, there is another hurricane barreling our way. Another disaster to be cleaned up. Another line to add to our to-do lists. It is natural for us to want to retreat into our classrooms, trying desperately to survive. It becomes us against our students, us against our administrations, us against the parents. It can all feel like a hindrance and annoyance when we are struggling to keep our heads above water.

Chad: *Thinking back to one of my early (and more difficult) years as an educator, I remember feeling like every email in my inbox or request from the office was a drain on my ability to "do my job." This included everything from requests for student work from parents to meetings after school to even specific needs or accommodations for students. Whether the requests were from parents, the administration, or my colleagues, they all got the same negative response of "Why won't you just leave me alone?"*

Looking back, this was the worst mindset I could have had. By placing myself against these stakeholders, I was already doomed to fail. Once this mindset had set in, every email, complaint, and student action became an act of war against my ability to do my job effectively.

The fact is, what I was really doing was making my job even more difficult. If I would have just asked any one of these stakeholders what their goal was, they would have probably said it was to help students succeed. We could have had a conversation and maybe figured out an efficient way to get information to them that allowed me to get back to my students. We could have worked together to help my students. If students, parents, administrators, and districts all have the same goal in mind, the same goal as teachers, why does it become so difficult to get on the same page?

This is why connecting and communicating effectively with these stakeholders becomes so important. When the entire community has the single goal of student achievement in mind, and it is clearly communicated, it greatly increases the chances of success for each student.

———————

Tiff: Seven years into my career and four years after having Amber in my class, I received a message from her through Facebook. She was then a sophomore in high school.

She told me that she'd struggled with depression and anxiety throughout middle school. She spent the first year of high school cutting herself and sank into such deep despair that she even contemplated taking her own life.

Those are hard words to read, and my teacher heart absolutely broke. She was my student in sixth grade, the very first year of middle school in our district. I knew at the time that she struggled, and I had hoped that in some way the time she spent in my classroom each day gave her a safe space where some of the stresses of her life could take a back seat for just a little while.

She went on to tell me that when her struggles first started in sixth grade, she did indeed treasure those mornings with me. That the openness of my room and my willingness to give her time each day meant the world to her. She told me that while she struggled for the next several years, my time with her continued to be a source of comfort and sanctuary. She said she thought of me often and wanted to tell me how much she appreciated the time I gave her.

———————

It is connecting with these students, with all their individual heartache, trauma, successes, and failures, that pushes us forward, fuels our passion, and inspires us to be better for the world. We propose that there are three aspects of connection that can change the way you and your students see education and learning in today's world:

- Connecting with students
- Connecting with stakeholders
- Connecting with each other

What follows are the tips and tricks that we have used ourselves. Some will feel comfortable to you; others won't. It isn't about using every suggestion here all at once or right away. You need to find what helps you be better for students. Try one out, reflect, and reevaluate. See what works and what doesn't, then just keep moving forward on your journey to better.

CONNECTING WITH STUDENTS

You may have heard the phrase "Maslow before Bloom" before. The idea is that before you are able to get at the recall, analysis, application, or evaluation of ideas, you must first ensure that students' most fundamental, basic needs are met. Do they feel safe? Do they feel heard? Have they had breakfast? Is their family struggling to make ends meet?

When Tiffany welcomed Amber into her classroom each morning, she was committing to focusing on what this child needed outside of the science and math content she was tasked to teach. Each student that walks through our doors has their own struggles and their own needs. But you know as well as we do that knowing each of your students on that level isn't always easy. It is hard enough when you have thirty students in an elementary-age classroom, and it's even harder when you teach high school with over two hundred students on your roster!

We don't have a magical rainbow unicorn solution that will allow you to snap your fingers and instantly build relationships with all of your students that help shape who they are as humans. There are college courses, countless education books, and nonstop dialogues throughout the education landscape about the importance of relationships with students, so we won't rehash all of the ideas here. What we do have, however, is a mindset shift we want to help you make that will peel back the layers of challenges blocking the path toward those relationships.

Consider the fact that the students sitting in our rooms every single day are quite possibly experiencing some of the hardest moments they have had yet in their lives. Sometimes, in our earnest rush to get through content, we completely miss—or worse, ignore—our students' struggles.

Our students are crying out, sometimes desperately, for connections with us. A kindergarten student who just wants to be close to you accidentally calls you mom and seems to always want you to clasp their sticky, germ-ridden, precious hand to connect. A middle school student showing up to your room twenty minutes before the start of the school day to help you organize books or on the pretense of wanting some extra practice problems probably wants to connect. A high school student who flops down at the desk in the back of your room, makes frequent, often inappropriate jokes, and rolls their eyes better than your own preteen daughter simply wants to connect.

If you believe, as we do, that students learn best in situations where they feel safe, heard, and supported, then you need a way to make sure that you don't miss these signals. You need to be able to see past your stack of papers and to-dos so you can see the connections your students are trying to make in their own unique—and sometimes odd—ways. But how? Try this idea:

———————

Tiff: Each morning when my alarm goes off (or, I should say, when my husband's alarm goes off, and he shoves me out of bed), I shuffle off to the kids' rooms to wake them, dress them, feed them, and then start the mommy taxi service from home to the babysitter's, where I drop Lincoln off, then on to Jeff's house where Kiya stays before school, then generally to the gas station where I get my daily dose of caffeine. In the ten-minute drive from there to school, I mentally walk through my day ahead.

- *Andrew just took an exam in history yesterday and is probably feeling pretty stressed this morning. Must make sure to take a minute to say hi to him when I see him on the way to first period.*
- *Evan is still recovering from his knee surgery and having trouble with chemistry. Maybe I will meet with him at lunch and bring him a piece of that candy he likes from my office.*
- *Sara and Carson both went through testing for ADHD last week and were late to one of my classes. Have to chat with them about how they feel about the testing they did. Oh yeah, and I have to make sure they are comfortable with the algebra equations we worked on too.*

Each one of my students gets a few seconds of mental time on my car ride. I am often not finished by the time I pull into my parking spot, but I always stay in my car until I have gone through my class roster for each class and mentally checked in on each student's well-being. Sometimes I take a few minutes to write myself a note on a Post-It to remind me of the connections I want to make with them.

I don't always remember to implement each of the ideas I plan during this time, but the simple act of thinking about and planning for my students' needs puts me in the mental mindset of what is most important in my job: the human beings that come into my classroom. Yes, I will be bombarded by emails and requests from the department chair. There will be grades to enter and lessons to plan. But by starting with my students and their needs, I start with what matters most—connecting with kids.

———————

How will you choose to focus on connections with students? How will you make sure that it is a priority and a routine that you build into your days? Take some time now and commit to something that you think will work for you. Write it down somewhere, tape it to your bathroom mirror, set an alarm on your phone. Take some action right now so that you start your days and your classes by connecting with your students first, then get to the content.

Connecting with students, understanding their needs, seeing them for who they are and what they want to be—these are all important! But students aren't the only ones we need to connect with.

CONNECTING WITH STAKEHOLDERS

You might design the most amazing lessons and units in history. Perhaps you can tell a story that pulls your students into new ideas, or you are a pro at pulling out those *Aha!* moments. Rock on! Good for you! But if the only audience you are aiming for with your brilliantly designed plans is students, you are missing out on some powerful connections that can make learning even more awesome for kids (and make your job far easier).

We are not the only adults that care about and influence the lives of the people sitting in our classrooms every day. Administrators want to ensure that every child has the chance to thrive and grow in a safe, welcoming environment while also making sure that all district, state, and national requirements and goals are met. Parents want to understand how their children are progressing, what is happening in the time a child spends in school, and what is expected of their kids and themselves. Community members want to know that schools are doing a good job developing kids into fully functioning adults who will enter the workforce well prepared to succeed and contribute to growth.

When the stresses of the job pile up and we find ourselves struggling to accomplish daily planning and grading, the idea of actively pursuing strong connections with these stakeholders is either forgotten or far too overwhelming to consider. The simple truth, though, is that we are making our jobs so much harder by neglecting to nurture these connections.

Consider these two scenarios, both occurring during parent–teacher conference night.

Scenario 1

Parents come in and, upon seeing the printout of benchmark testing that you are required to distribute, are immediately concerned. They express dismay at their child's progress and confusion about what the content is that their student doesn't understand, how long this has been going on, and why on Earth they didn't know there was a problem earlier. You respond by mentioning that the class gradebook is available online, and they immediately become even more frustrated.

Eventually, the parents inform you that they will be contacting administration and will be seeking a classroom switch for their child. The next day, right on cue, the principal comes to your room before school starts and discusses the situation with you. You are taken aback that they, too, seem irritated with you.

Scenario 2

Parents of your student come in and, upon seeing the printout of benchmark testing that you are required to distribute, say they already have the copy you sent home two weeks ago and appreciated your follow-up phone call about the results. They are well-versed in the systems and routines of your classroom and know what kinds of questions to ask their child about their day because of your regularly distributed newsletters, emails, and up-to-date online photo album.

On their way out of the building, those parents pass the principal and comment on how glad they are that their child is in your class. They feel informed and connected to what is happening in the classroom.

Okay. Obviously, these are two examples taken to the extremes, but the contrast between them is really the take-home message. You need to make a choice and, just like all the other choices we have asked you to make, it is one born of the Teach Better mindset. Be better today than you were yesterday and be better tomorrow than you were today. It's also important to understand that if you do not choose to actively work toward Scenario 2, then you are automatically choosing Scenario 1.

Chad: *A great example of what not to do happened early in my career. I was swamped with planning, meetings, and responsibilities, so my parent communication suffered. The weekly emails, class site updates, calls home, and positive notes just seemed to fall by the wayside. When parent–teacher conferences came up, I had a parent ask me why I hadn't let them know how much their child was struggling. As I sat there, I didn't have a good reason other than . . . I just hadn't done. A simple email or phone call earlier in the semester could have helped me utilize the parent as a resource to support the child. This is a mistake I never let myself make again.*

Just like each shift you make in your journey to teaching better, connecting better is all about reflection first. Chad could easily have blamed parents, saying they weren't engaged enough in their children's lives—how could they not know their children were struggling? He could have blamed his principal or the central office for the new initiatives this year or common assessments that are now required and taking up so much of his time. He could have blamed students for not communicating with their parents or not putting in the work necessary to learn what they needed to learn.

It is so easy, so automatic, for us to look outside of ourselves to explain why things aren't going well in our lives. To actually make things better, we need to be willing to turn the mirror on ourselves and be prepared to find the ways we can improve, not wish for ways other people could.

After you have taken that time to reflect, at some point you need the actual strategies to make those connections happen. There are thousands of different ideas you could try, and it can take some trial and error to find a strategy that works for you with your unique students and your unique administration and your unique community. Let's take a few minutes to explore our top four favorite strategies for connecting with stakeholders.

1. Tech Tools to Connect

Living and teaching in the twenty-first century is pretty awesome. New websites, apps, devices, and tech tools come out all the time! We are fortunate to be a part of an incredible surge of technology resources designed specifically for education. The drawbacks? As soon as you learn one new tool, another one comes along to learn! Filtering through the insane amount of options for technology integration and actually finding high-quality, easy, and effective learning tools can seem like hunting for a needle in a haystack!

There are a few tools right now that are effective, such as Remind and Seesaw, though we acknowledge that by the time you are reading this book, there are likely to be new, perhaps better options. Blogs are a good way to communicate information to parents, and the students in your class can contribute to it too.

ARE YOU USING TECHNOLOGY EFFECTIVELY?

Using tech in education isn't about finding cool new tech tools. It's about effectively integrating those tools into your classroom for maximum impact. Learn more about effective technology integration at Teachbetter.com/ BookResources

Tiff: I had a plan! Having just started my master's degree in instructional technology, my mind was just overflowing with ideas for new tech tools to use and ways it was going to be awesome to be a student in my class and to be the parent of a student in my class!

Enter: The classroom blog.

Oh, what great dreams I had of this absolutely amazing digital record of the fabulous learning my classes would do. Parents would check it all the time, share it with grandparents, and send me countless emails about how awesome I was.

It. Would. Be. Epic.

But then it wasn't.

We started out well. I took pictures on the first day of school and posted about what we did and then shared the link via email to parents. I filmed a neat science demonstration the next week and added a blog post about that. Two months in, I realized I hadn't posted anything to the blog in weeks and had never received any feedback from parents about how great it was to see their child on the blog. When I checked the back end of my blog website, I saw that the site had been visited exactly eight times—in two months.

Whatever tech tool you decide to implement, don't make the same mistakes Tiffany did. Follow these guidelines and you will be on a good path to tech that actually connects with others in the way you want it to!

T: Take yourself out of the equation (at least a little bit). Recruit the students sitting in your class to be a part of using whatever tech tool you choose. If you're an elementary school teacher, make "photographer" a classroom job. You could even have a copywriter job, in which a student writes a couple sentences about what was done in class that day. Middle or high school teacher? You can put even more responsibility on your students. Assign a weekly or monthly review as a recurring class assignment, where students spend fifteen minutes in a small group writing a summary of the week, finding relevant external links, and inserting images into a blog post. If you try to do all the work to connect with home, not only will you make your job more difficult, you will be missing out on great opportunities for students to learn skills that will serve them well for years to come.

E: Everyone is invited. Whatever tech tool you choose to support connection, make sure you invite all stakeholders to be involved. Often, we think of parents first when we talk about stakeholder connections, but your administrator shouldn't be left out. Invite them to your Remind account. Send them emails about new posts in your class blog. Invite them to be a guest photographer in your classroom. The more connected they are, the more they will support you in your efforts.

C: Consistency is key. Tiffany made this critical error with her first attempt at a blog and wound up two months into the year with very little content and almost no connection. If you are committing to connecting better with stakeholders this year (and you should be!), take out your calendar right now and pencil in (or type in) specific due dates for yourself with tasks to connect in some way through your digital tool.

August 28th—Record first day of school video and post to class blog. Email parents the link.

September 5th—Student-designed science experiment today. Have students take pictures and post them to blog.

September 18th—Share examples of student writing in an anthology-style blog post. Send parents link again and remind them about the blog.

September 24th—Class picture day is tomorrow! Post your most awkward school picture to get a good giggle from everyone.

You get the idea, right? Plan out what your connections will be and hold yourself accountable to them!

H: Have fun with it! We can personally guarantee you that at some point in your efforts to integrate technology in ways that support deeper connections, something will go wrong. You will forget something you planned to do. A parent might not want their child's picture shared online. You may be in the middle of a collaborative class blog when the Wi-Fi goes down.

Something will go wrong. The best thing you can do in the face of these tech challenges? Laugh, smile, have fun! Demonstrate to your students that you are a continuously evolving human who doesn't get everything right immediately, and everyone knows that Wi-Fi magically fails at the absolute worst time.

Beyond smiling in the face of tech challenges, reframe the way you think about these connections. District making you use a class webpage this year? Use it as an opportunity to break the ice with students by throwing in some of your most awkward childhood photos. Feel like you need to use that new parent connection app that everyone else is using? See it not as a burden, but as an opportunity!

2. Kill Some Trees with Paper

Yes, trees are important, and preventing deforestation is good. No, you should not make one hundred copies of a map of Europe for your class, realize you want a different one, and throw the original hundred away.

Sometimes, however, you simply cannot beat paper. One of those times is when you are trying to build connections. Sending home weekly or monthly newsletters is a good start, and if you aren't doing so, it's definitely something to consider. But there is one thing you can do with paper that just can't be equaled in any other medium: write a note.

———

Rae: *Each year, I strive to send a minimum of one postcard home to every student in my classroom. Even with 180 school days, one note per student can be a tedious and time-consuming task. I remember setting a goal for myself to write one note a day—or five a week—to help accomplish my goal.*

Seeming successful as I worked on this mission, I was able to send a minimum of two notes home in the mail to students and their families, celebrating their successes throughout the year and their impact on me and the classroom. I had no idea the true meaning of these silly notes.

Since the start of this goal, I continually hear from students through the year: "I got your note at home yesterday!" or "I got your Postcard Mrs. Hughart! It's now up on my fridge!" I must assume, however, that once May comes along, families complete a spring cleaning, taking my small messages and placing them in the trash. We've all been there, and I get it!

A few years later, I bumped into an old student at Target with his mother and younger sister. Shocked to be bumping into a family (while I am in my teacher summer outfit, shorts and a raggedy shirt), I began to catch up with them and ask how high school was going. Not quite understanding the mother and son's conversation as they continued to bicker back and forth, pointing to his wallet, the student looked at me and said, "I actually still have this", then he pulled out my postcard, folded into fourths, from his wallet.

I think my chin hit the tile below my feet. I was absolutely speechless. His mother joked that he had kept it in his wallet since middle school to remind him of the awesome time he'd had with some of his favorite teachers.

———

You never know how one small action you take to celebrate a student's success can impact them. Would Rae's student have kept an email for years? Would he have printed it out and stuck it in his wallet as a reminder of teachers that actually made a difference for him? Probably not.

As you strive to improve the ways you connect with all the stakeholders in your life as a teacher, make a commitment to break out some paper and a pen and jot a simple note. Email is a great tool for rapid, easy communication, but mailing a handwritten note honestly can't be beat. Sure, you will still send updates and questions via email, but taking the time to write out a message to someone tells them that you really care. It shows them that you are willing to take time out of your life and busy day to communicate with them on a more personal level.

Another benefit to paper? It is unusual! Because the world is so digitized today, actually receiving a handwritten note is a rare occurrence. Its uniqueness makes its impact more powerful. An email can be read, dismissed, and forgotten in an instant, but a piece of paper with your handwriting on it makes the brain sit up and think, *Oh! Weird! This is unique, so I'd better pay attention to it.*

Who should you write notes to, and what should they say? The list could be endless, but here are some thoughts to get you started:

"Thanks for your support this morning at the team meeting!" jotted on a Post-It note and stuck on a colleague's computer while they are taking their students to specials.

"Joey really contributed well to our class discussion today. He really moved the conversation about fractions forward!" written on a blank card and mailed after school.

"I'd love for you to come in and see my class exploring ecosystems on Wednesday! Can you make it?" on a half sheet of paper put in your administrator's mailbox.

Sure, writing notes is a great idea, but how do you actually make sure it happens and fits into your daily routine? It's all about creating a routine and structure that will make this communication painless and impossible to forget. Try these ideas:

- Pick up a box of blank notecards and, on the first day of school, have every student write their home address on four envelopes and put stamps on them. Collect them, shuffle them up, and place them back in the box sitting on your desk. At the end of every day, take an envelope out, write a super quick note to the student or the parents of the student and send it off. Removing the barriers to this process by pre-addressing and stamping all the envelopes gives you one less excuse to put off the task!

- Keep a set of Post-It notes and a pen in your school mailbox. Each day when you pick up your mail, take a Post-It note and jot down a quick message for a colleague. It could be a thank you, an idea for collaboration, or a thought pertinent to some life event they have recently experienced. Pop it in their mailbox and boom, connection made!

- Keep a notebook on your desk and, at the end of every week, write a handwritten letter to a student and their family. Shoot for a couple of paragraphs that focus on the positive, such as what the student has done well this month, how they have improved, and what you appreciate about them. Mail it out that day and watch the positivity spread. Determine how many letters you would need to write each week to get one to every student you teach by the end of the year so you make sure nobody gets left out!

3. Video is your friend

Have you ever opened your email, seen a message with four to five paragraphs, and immediately gotten a sinking feeling in your stomach? Let's be honest, we all get hundreds of emails every day, and if one requires significant mental effort to read, understand, and respond to, it frequently gets put off. That isn't what we want to happen when we are working to build connections with stakeholders!

We also know that sometimes you have to communicate information that takes more than a few paragraphs to explain, so what do you do?

Sit down and make a video. When people are inundated daily with thousands of words and hundreds of messages, your words get lost in the shuffle. But a video of you sitting in your class, talking about what students are learning or working on is much easier for a stakeholder to consume than reading five paragraphs. The purpose of recording and sending videos is to make it as easy as humanly

RECORDING YOUR OWN VIDEOS?

There are so many great tools for recording content to share with parents, students, and the community. Not sure how to get started? Check out the tutorial videos at teachbetter.com/ BookResources possible for the people important in the growth, learning, and development of the students in your class to get information about and form connections with the work happening in your classroom.

Now, we know that some of you are probably reacting with shock and horror: "You mean you want me to record a video of myself and send it to people? I hate the way my voice sounds on video. It is so awkward!" It's time to get over that and just do it anyway!

———————

Tiff: *I love sending video messages home! I discovered screencasting a while back when I decided to start flipping my classroom (delivering instruction out of class, perhaps as video or reading assignments, and then further exploring and clarifying the content during class). Initially, I just recorded videos for my students, and after I got over my initial shock about how I sounded on video, I was able to see that their engagement with the videos I created was much higher than it was when I gave them typed explanations or examples. They loved being able to repeatedly rewatch videos if they had trouble understanding, and they said watching me explain content helped them understand better than reading an explanation, which was okay with me because I wasn't teaching them how to read; I was teaching them math and science!*

Eventually, I thought to myself, If the students love it so much, maybe their parents will too! I sat down that afternoon and recorded my first-ever video for parents. (I should say, I recorded five versions of my first video for parents. The perfectionist in me took over!) I knew that many of my students' parents did not like the "new way" we were teaching math because they didn't understand it, and they were openly hostile when their students talked about the math at home. Well, you can imagine the impact that had on my students' opinions of math. It was not good.

The video was short, just three and a half minutes long, and it was a quick explanation of how we solved multi-digit multiplication problems using an area model. I explained the ways this model for multiplication helped students understand how numbers work and how it would eventually lead to an understanding of the traditional algorithm for multiplication (the way most parents learned how to multiply).

I uploaded the video to YouTube, sent an email with the video embedded, and waited for fireworks of awesomeness to go off.

No, I didn't have sixty parents emailing me back about how great my video was and how much they loved the new math approaches we were using, but I did have a couple parents reply back either requesting clarification or just sending a quick thank you. I tracked my YouTube video stats and saw that the video was getting views! My video was at least helping someone. And that mattered.

Tiffany went on to create videos regularly, both for her students and for their parents. She even started recording videos to explain a tech tool to a colleague who asked her to demonstrate how she set up her grade book to support a standards-based approach. Weekly newsletter or weekly video? The video is likely to be watched and interacted with more than the newsletter a parent might find shoved in a student's backpack months later.

––––––––

One other quick note about these videos. Make sure to copy your administration on the video messages you send or invite them to subscribe to your YouTube channel, where you post these videos. Remember, connecting well with stakeholders goes beyond connecting with parents. Colleagues and administrators who understand what you are doing in your classroom are more likely to support your efforts.

4. Pick up the phone

Whether you love chatting on the phone or almost always send calls to voicemail, making a call to a stakeholder is something you must make time to do in your busy teacher life. Even if a parent never answers the phone, you should still call. Even if a local business doesn't call you back or won't support your classroom project, you should still call. The fact that you attempted to communicate and were willing to take the time to call can start the process of building positive, productive connections.

––––––––

Rae: *Let's talk about my love–hate relationship with phone calls. Throughout my career, I have seen it all . . .*

- *phone calls that went smoothly*
- *phone calls that made me cry*
- *phone calls resulting in another call to my administration*
- *phone calls that broke a relationship*
- *phone calls that built a stronger relationship*
- *phone calls ending with a full voicemail box*

While the negative phone calls more readily come to mind when thinking of a sto-
ry related to picking up the phone as an educator, the negative phone calls are not
the ones you should choose to give weight in your life.

Years ago, one of my students, Luna, was struggling and continued to find a dis-
connect in learning. She scored high on standardized tests and low on unit assess-
ments. She seemed scared to speak up in class, and even when I was working with
her one on one, day after day, she didn't seem to retain information well at all.
Every day felt like starting over. To most, she was a mystery.

I called her mother one afternoon during my planning period after working with
Luna in math class to talk through what I was seeing in the classroom. To be hon-
est, I was curious as to whether she needed specialized support, as I saw faint sim-
ilarities in her inconsistency retaining information to my own learning journey.
Her mother was overjoyed to hear from me, and she relayed similar concerns for
what she saw at home.

As we chatted, her mother told story after story of her witnessing the same man-
nerisms during home chore tasks and conversations around the dinner table.
Shocked to hear the similarities taking place at home and at school, we began to
discuss mental health.

"She always seems very nervous in class," I said. "Nevertheless, it seems Luna and
I have a wonderful relationship with each other. I am not sure what is making her
so worried to speak to me."

"We see the same at home," her mother responded. "One moment she is bubbly
and then we see a huge shift in her mannerisms."

Her mother and I spoke regularly for months, tracking behaviors, poring over
Luna's academic data, and consulting with other experts in the community. Ulti-
mately, we learned Luna was suffering from massive anxiety, but no one knew.

To put it all into context, now Luna is a successful high school student who contin-
ues to see an outside therapist twice a week. She just visited my classroom earlier
this semester to say hello and update me on her new dreams and plans for college.
She also (getting a little choked up here) brought her precalculus semester report
card to me during her last visit. She'd received an awesome, shining B+!

I would love to think that her seventh- or eighth-grade teachers would have helped
get to the bottom of Luna's struggles if I had not picked up the phone that day—and
they might have—but I am so glad I chose to be a part of Luna's journey. I am so
glad I chose to pick up the phone and make that phone call.

———

As you take the steps to make sure the adults in your students' lives are connected, informed, and included in what happens in your classroom, you will run into hiccups. Your video won't load, the handwritten letter you sent was never opened, your new favorite tech tool gets an update and then just doesn't work as well anymore. Come back to the Teach Better mindset and remember you do not have to be perfect. Everything you try does not have to go perfectly. Remind yourself that the goal of education is to help young people grow and develop into adulthood.

Sure, you might get frustrated with that parent who seems to always find something wrong with what you do, and the idea of communicating more frequently with them might make you nervous. It might be really difficult to see how that last-minute request, email, or meeting with your administrator is helping you teach better, and you may feel like avoiding additional contact with them.

By ensuring that all stakeholders are informed and that you are clearly communicating your instruction, expectations, and perspective, you are not only avoiding unnecessary emails, you're building a team to support what matters: student growth and learning.

CONNECTING WITH EACH OTHER

Whether you realize it or not, you're lucky to be teaching at this moment in history. We are all riding along on this education journey at a time that is unlike any other in several centuries. Throughout history, there have been a handful of events that have completely disrupted the status quo in human interaction, learning, and society—and we are living in one right now.

An agricultural revolution, launching across the globe in 10,000 BC, shifted humanity from a nomadic lifestyle to one of stationary communities. This shift allowed humans to focus more time on experimentation and innovation, more food to allow the population to expand, and the ability to have long-lasting societies that focused on more than just survival.

The written word is something we take for granted today, but for much of human history it was not even a glimmer of an idea. Between 5,000 and 2,000 BC, humans began to use symbols to represent ideas and letters, words, sentences, and paragraphs, and more followed. The ability to share an idea with another person in a different area shifted humanity again, connecting us in ways never before imagined.

The Gutenberg press, a brilliant invention from the 1400s, which allowed books to be printed in mass quantities rather than copied laboriously by individual monks, opened the world to the written word. For the first time, the written word could be shared with the masses rather than being reserved for a handful of religious and political leaders. The Gutenberg press led directly to the reformation that rocked the religious and political world. It launched the Renaissance and changed the human learning experience forever.

Throughout the twentieth century, a series of events occurred that would again change the face of humanity forever. Complex machines with digital information storage ability burst into existence in the thirties and forties and then into our homes with the advent of the personal computer in the seventies and eighties. Floppy disks and *Oregon Trail* made their way into schools in the late eighties and then, in what seemed like the blink of an eye, everything changed again.

The time? November 1990. The place? The European Organization for Nuclear Research (CERN). The person? Tim Berners-Lee. The idea? A "World Wide Web" accessed through computing devices and open to all. A portal for sharing information on a scale unimaginable for almost all of human history.

The internet arrived and changed everything. Within a decade, many schools in the country had internet-connected computer labs. By the end of 2017, 94 percent of schools in the United States had high-speed internet connections, with the percentage growing constantly through nonprofit and government grant programs.

What a different world we live in now.

It is a different world for our students than it was for us. It is a different world today than it was just five years ago. And the journey we take as educators striving to be better for our students is different than it ever has been.

At no other time in human history has connecting with new ideas, education leaders, and an army of other educators been easier. As teachers, we used to be limited to the people working in our districts, the colleagues in our school, or the teacher down the hallway. Now, in an instant, we can hop on to social media and connect with educators across the globe who can support and challenge us and help us grow.

We are no longer alone.

————

Rae: I had a lot of goals after I finally decided to become a teacher. Number one, become a Redbird at Illinois State University. Number two, become the teacher who could finally explain why learning math was beneficial and attainable for any student. Number three, get my master's degree.

As a struggling student, unsure I would even be accepted into an undergraduate program, I set the goal of earning my master's just to say I could. I felt it was a badge of honor. A certificate of my intelligence. Ignorant of the fact that most educators end up with a master's at some point in their career, this was my goal!

When I found myself in a school district that offered a tuition waiver for furthering education, I began my master's program three years into my teaching career. I had no idea what topic I wanted to focus on, outside of the generic "Curriculum and Instruction" bracket; therefore, outside of the required course work, I essentially closed my eyes and played "eeny, meeny, miny, moe" to select my elective classes.

I somehow ended up on a technology track, completing course after course on tech integration and classroom technology implementation; however, no matter how diligent I was, I discovered my last semester that I was one class shy of graduating. Crap.

I did what any good student would do: I signed up for the first available course I could get into to still graduate on time: "432 Technology across the Disciplines." While I was not thrilled to be doubling up course work right before graduation, the class was taught by one of my favorite professors, so it felt as close to a win–win as possible.

During the course, I was required to build a Professional Learning Network (PLN). For the sake of getting that master's in my hands by May, I created my first Twitter account in March 2016.

I have vivid memories of logging on occasionally, scrolling through my feed, and questioning why in the world Twitter existed. Why should I care what Trump is tweeting about? How do you follow any conversations between educators if you only see a 140-character snapshot? And what on Earth is a hashtag?

Here I was at the tail end of my master's, just two courses away from my degree, and I felt lost and confused all over again.

I hated Twitter.

Then the assignment arrived from my professor . . .

Week 6: "Everyone must participate in a Twitter chat."

If it would be possible to insert a gif in this book, it would be the image of Kevin McCallister (Macaulay Culkin) from Home Alone with his hands against his face and mouth open wide . . . "Ahh!"

———

Well, for the sake of the grade, Rae did it. She mustered up her energy and prepared to dive in to her first-ever Twitter chat, and she wasn't too thrilled about it. What hashtag did she choose to follow for her checkmark on the "join a Twitter chat" assignment? #TLAP

Rae: I remember getting involved in this chat without even realizing the popular #TLAP hashtag was an acronym for Dave Burgess's book, Teach Like a Pirate, which I so admired. I joined in for my first chat and found myself joining again and again and again. Each week I learned something new and made new connections. I discovered ideas that matched my own philosophies and others that challenged the long-held beliefs I had about teaching and learning.

During one of these early chats, Dave Burgess himself sent me a direct message about being a new participant. I remember being incredibly starstruck, trying to play it cool while one my favorite educational authors was messaging me.

Trust me, I can actually explain what this felt like. Remember when you were in middle school and the person you liked sent you a two-word text message? Your heart dropped into your stomach and your hands began to sweat. Regardless of how smooth you were before, now you could barely form a full sentence, rereading and deleting every possible response.

Well, it was nothing like that. I was as cool as a cucumber . . . (insert eye roll)

Unaware of the incredulous shock I felt on my end of the computer, Dave asked me if I would be open to hosting a #TLAP chat. Little did I know, hosting this Twitter chat was about to lead to a life-changing connection.

No, not meeting my husband! That had happened three years prior! But I sure did get to meet one cool dude—Mr. Jeff Gargas!

Twitter is not the end all, be all of connecting with others in the education world, but the impact it has had on the global education community is stunning, and it continues to grow. In our admittedly unscientific exploration into the effects of Twitter participation on educator growth, the correlation is too strong to ignore. Educator after educator after educator has shared stories with us about how their professional

INTIMIDATED BY TWITTER CHATS?

Get started and check out our favorite chats at Teachbetter.com/BookResources

growth after engaging with other educators through social media is unmatched by any other time in their careers. It is more impactful than their undergraduate teaching degrees, more significant than the required weekly team meetings at school, and more helpful than any textbook they have read.

Cognitive dissonance, the challenging of our long-held understanding and beliefs with contradicting information, can be a powerful tool for learning, and it is something that can be found when you interact with other educators with different experiences, insights, and ideas.

————————

Rae: *To actually tell the story of how meeting Jeff went, I scrolled all the way back in my messages on Twitter to share the actual conversation.*

As a newbie to Twitter, I had this cool message I sent every new follower to thank them for connecting. I sent that same generic message to @TheGridMethod handle (now @TeachBetterTeam).

Shocked to receive a response from this huge education company, they encouraged me to check out their website, Facebook group, and (at the time) single online course. As the polite, busy teacher I am, I thanked them for the information and put it at the bottom of my to-do list.

Then, who showed up in our conversation, but the awesome Mr. Jeff Gargas . . .

 Hey Rae! Jeff here. I'd love to connect and learn more about TeachFurther. It sounds pretty awesome. Can we connect via email? Jeff@thegridmethod.com

1 Apr 2017

I remember thinking, Really? The website was not enough? I don't have time for a sales pitch today from some education company trying to sell products to poor teachers. *But having still not mastered the word no, I sent Jeff an email.*

Jeff let me talk on and on about the Teach Further Model, something I was passionate about down to my core. I had a free, self-made website on which I shared links, wrote stories about the impact I was having on students, and shared my experiences in the classroom.

Then came what I thought to be the dreaded sales pitch I always knew was headed my way: "Our mission is pretty simple: Help teachers reach more students. Let's

jump on a call sometime this week, if you're available."

Recognizing I was in no position to spend the fifty cents left from my paycheck last week to purchase something for my classroom, I sent Jeff a time or two I could connect, noting that I was not in a position to purchase anything. Jeff must have thought that was pretty funny when he responded back to my email confirming time zones and telling me he didn't want my money.

Once I hopped on that call with Jeff and Chad, I vividly remember thinking, These guys are crazy. *They talked on and on about the impact Mastery Learning was having in classrooms across the country. They told me about their insane travel schedule and the data they had collected along the way to prove the change necessary in education to shift toward teachers focusing on self-paced, personalized classrooms.*

To be honest, friends, it was not that I disagreed with their vision; I just truly believed I had tried it all already. I had done flipped classroom. I had done "choice assignments." I had done differentiation. And while I chose to implement some of it in my classroom from time to time, I had also experienced the pitfalls that come with these systems; the day you walk in and the internet is down, the student that does not do work outside of class, the student you don't know how to reach. Although the ideal classroom they described sounded good, I felt it was unrealistic and unattainable.

This may have been the last time in my life when I, without trying it first, shut down another educator's ideas. After they challenged me to try the mastery framework, I had to put my foot in my mouth. It changed my life, and I could never go back to the way I was facilitating my classroom before. Not because I didn't want to, but because my students would never let me go back again.

They loved it. They wanted it. They were eager for it.

And even though I had so much confidence in my classroom already, prior to meeting Jeff and Chad, I knew my students were better with this framework. So I took this tool and all the other pieces I was already doing that were also best for students, and I implemented them and overlaid them on one another for the rest of my career.

———

Putting ourselves in a position where we are challenged with new ideas can, if we allow it, propel us on paths forward that we never anticipated. Our willingness to consider change and openness to growth is, we believe, the number one most important characteristic we can possess as educators. Rae took a risk, took a leap, and decided to try something because of a connection she made with the larger world of education. Will you take the same leap?

If Twitter isn't your thing, and social media makes you cringe, you can still achieve this level of connection and growth if you actively search outside your own experience and outside the four walls of your classroom.

––––––––––

Tiff: When my sister was in high school, she struggled with some pretty crippling anxiety. I vividly remember, however, when she decided that she was not going to let that anxiety rule her life. She made a decision that in order to conquer this fear, she would do something every day that scared her. This could have been a small challenge, like taking a risk on a class assignment, or a much greater challenge, like submitting her college application. No matter what, my sister made it her mission to push herself every single day despite ambiguity and fear.

Seeing her make this decision and struggle through her fears had a great impact on me as a developing young person. It is to her that I owe a large chunk of my success as a teacher.

I remember the first time I truly took her philosophy to heart as an educator. I had been teaching for several years and found myself in a new position as a seventh-grade math teacher. A few weeks before the school year started, I had a colleague tell me about a video they'd watched on YouTube about some teachers in Colorado (Jonathan Bergman and Aaron Sams) who were playing around with a concept called "flipped learning" and the "flipped classroom."

I took some time to watch the video she sent me and then do some more digging online. I read blogs and watched videos of classrooms using a flipped model. As a math teacher, I thought this could be the perfect way for me to have more time to work one-on-one and in small groups with my students to help them with their struggles and push them further when they needed it.

This was only two weeks before the school year started. Conventional wisdom told me I should take more time to sort out the decisions. Not being a big fan of conventional wisdom, I chose to ignore this advice. I made a decision despite my fear of failure and lack of experience with flipping a class and despite my lack of knowledge on how to create video lectures for my students to watch at home.

I decided I was going to leap.

I dove into this adventure wholeheartedly and flipped every single math class I taught that year, both general education math and honors math. I stumbled my way through it, spending a significant amount of time recording and rerecording videos. My students and I learned together how to make a flipped classroom work. I saw unbelievable growth in my learners not only in their academic progress but also in their enthusiasm for learning! I leaped before I looked. I did not have it all planned out. I had no idea the specifics of how I was going to make it work. But I knew it was good education practice, and I knew that it would make a difference in my students' learning.

––––––––

When we take the time to forge, nourish, and engage in connections with others, we expand our world in ways we can't anticipate. We have talked a lot about connecting digitally with other educators, primarily because that has been such a source of inspiration and learning for each of us here!

Let's not forget, however, the power of a face-to-face, nurtured, and sustained connection with another human. Jeff is probably the best example we know of someone who is an absolute rock star at building and sustaining this kind of connection. We often call him the "connector" of the team. He always seems to know someone who can support an idea or solve any problem anyone is having. He is a better networker than anyone else we know. And the best part? All of it comes from a place of him genuinely being interested in people's' stories and caring about their lives.

––––––––

Jeff: *I met this guy named Fred. He came into the Caribou Coffee I managed, wearing Hiram College soccer gear, and I decided that I was going to be the one serving him coffee. Hiram is where my wife, Amy, had graduated from, so I asked him whether he played or coached the team there.*

He told me that he was just running a camp there for high school kids but mentioned that he was the assistant coach at Lake High School. We got to talking, and he mentioned they needed a freshman coach. One thing led to another, and I ended up getting that job, which, interestingly, is what helped Chad and me connect on a deeper level. (This was all before Teach Better.)

Until then, Chad and I knew each other because I used to manage his band, and, to be honest, that relationship didn't end super smoothly. But I knew that Chad had been a goalie in college, so I decided to ask him to come work with my goalies. Through this, we discovered a shared intense love for Chinese buffets, and we actually became friends.

We forged a friendship, and at one point down the road, I reached out to have him review a business card design I had. A little while after that, I shared my e-book with him for feedback. When Chad was toying with the idea of creating an e-book, he called the only person he knew who had published one: me.

———————

Jeff built a casual relationship with Fred over a cup of coffee and a shared love of soccer. This led to a job coaching soccer and a renewed connection with Chad (nothing having to do with education). A business card, an e-book, a phone call, and a company later, and that small cup of coffee led him to this moment with this team and sharing our story with you.

COMMIT AND CONNECT

We do not know where our connections will lead. Just as we may never know the impact of our smile on a child's day or the effect of a Post-It note in a colleague's mailbox, we cannot possibly predict the direction our connections will take us. One of Tiffany's daughters, Rachel, used to love a song by Avicii called "Wake Me Up." In this song, there is a lyric that always made Tiffany pause and reflect: "I can't tell where the journey will end, but I know where to start."

Start your journey with connections. We cannot predict where they will take you, but we guarantee they will challenge you, help you grow, and, potentially, change your life.

Make the decision and commit to connecting in some way today, this week, this month, this year. Don't try to tackle all of the suggestions here at once. Let's face it, you are probably not Superman with superhuman strength and stamina; instead, be like the tortoise from the classic fable "The Tortoise and the Hare." Slow and steady wins the race. Don't stop; don't move backward. Don't close yourself off or brush connections away as something that is just too challenging to maintain.

>COFFEE WITH THE PRINCIPAL: BRYAN ZWEMKE (@BRYANZWEMKE)
High school principal, Illinois

As a principal, I am in awe of the way teachers can make connections with students and parents. They are masterful at learning about their families, areas of strength, and challenges. My role as principal is to create an environment where forming those relationships is just as important as academic growth. I continually look for ways to form authentic relationships with students and families; my favorite way, though, is "Coffee with the Principal."

"Coffee with the Principal" is nothing more than an intentional opportunity, every six weeks, for parents to meet with building administration and the rest of my outstanding staff to ask questions, provide feedback, and network. Questions about curriculum, safety, technology, communication, social emotional learning, clubs, and middle-level education—you name it, we answer it!

Why take the time away from other administrative tasks to ensure this is done consistently? Because a building is more than a space for learning; it is a space to connect better and form real relationships with our families. Once a part of our middle school family, always a part of our family.

We host this event a number of different ways throughout the year to best support building these relationships. I host two Coffees specifically with parents of students with special needs, with our Assistant Director of Student Services, and with others that can be team or grade level specific.

My favorite and most attended Coffees continue to be with new incoming families. While this event always begins with anxious parents and students entering the room concerned with the big transition they are about to embark on while becoming a new middle school student, it always concludes filled with excitement for the new year!

Making this shift from anxiety driven to enthusiastic is a strategic balance of listening and sharing information. We always begin this event the same way, focused on self-awareness. I ask parents to rate themselves on how they feel about their child transitioning from a small elementary school to a middle school with over 1,400 students on a scale of one to five.

Next, we move through the typical logistical questions:
- What type of homework does a student get in the middle school?
- How do you manage use of the Chromebook the school gives?
- How do I buy a PE uniform?
- How does a parent pick up work?

- Where do you rent an instrument?
- How long does it take for a student to figure out their locker?
- Are cell phones allowed in the school?

From my perspective, these questions have easy, simple answers, but beyond that, parents are looking for reassurance. For this Coffee, I bring in eighth-grade student leaders to serve on a panel and veteran middle school parents to answer these questions and engage in their shared experience. They sit with the new families and answer their questions. Seeing a thirteen-year-old child reassure a first-time middle school parent is heart-warming.

Then the fun begins. Everyone in attendance plays a game I like to call "Best Hopes, Worst Fears." This game is full of laughter as parents paint a picture of their experiences in middle school as well as tearful reflection on their children growing up too fast. Even through the mixed emotion, I am reju-venated by witnessing our parents share in community with one another, forming new connections and friendships and problem-solving as a middle school family to answer questions, together.

As I now have middle school children of my own, I have recognized that these were the questions my own child had. Curriculum questions were rarely asked and were saved for Curriculum Night. These sessions were about cre-ating a sense of belonging. These surface-level questions often have to be looked at from the perspective of the question behind the question. In other words, all parents want is a safe environment for their child, where they are secure, prepared, and happy. There's no question about that.

The relationships formed with these families who come to the Coffees on a consistent basis have lasted through their child's middle school experience. They often check in at sporting events, concerts, or while at the school drop-ping off an item their child may have forgotten. During those encounters, I know we are furthering the connection our middle school family works to build each and every day.

Communication is often at the center of every great problem and every great solution. But it is only with connecting better with our middle school family members that communication is able to blossom inside our building.

CHAPTER 4
ENGAGE BETTER

"OUR KIDS DO NOT WANT TO BE TAUGHT, THEY WANT TO BE MOVED . . . . FOCUS A LITTLE LESS ON FIGURING OUT HOW YOU WILL TEACH THEM, AND A LITTLE MORE ON HOW YOU WILL INSPIRE THEM."

–PAUL BOGUSH

Students crowd the door, ready to pile into the classroom before the bell rings. They throw a quick smile at you when you greet them outside the door and say "Hi," but they are clearly in a rush to slide on past you. As the bell rings, you step through the doorway and see a small group of students sitting on the windowsill chatting, someone off in the corner on their phone, and a few others reading books. Two students appear to be drawing something in a notebook, and another is using the whiteboards and markers that you always have tucked away on a bookshelf.

Sound familiar?

What if we told you that the students on the windowsill are debating the meaning of the results from an experiment they designed and executed last class? The one on the phone is scheduling a Google Hangout for the class to interview the scientist from NASA that he emailed last week. The books the students are reading include a memoir, a biography, a textbook, and an anthology of poetry, all connected to the topic of global warming. And the students using the whiteboards? One is explaining the impact of greenhouse gases to the other, using drawings.

A pipe dream, you say? Disbelief wouldn't be an unusual response at this moment. Even we have, at times, wondered if the ideal of a fully engaged, interested, and actively learning student body is actually possible. But we have seen it. We've been in classrooms around the country that have created this utopian vision of what a classroom could be . . . what a classroom should be.

What does it take to get there?

First, we have to redefine our goals as educators and our goals for students.

THE GOAL OF EDUCATION

A common understanding and goal of education is that our students will go through the school system to then take on a role participating in their community. We would like to offer an alternative perspective.

What if we shifted the conversation from how many students grow up to be a productive part of their community to how many students grow up to be transformative change agents in it? What if we could help a generation of young people develop into caring, compassionate, invested, and driven participants in, and active builders of, the communities in which they live?

Educators dream of these outcomes, but that dream quickly gets buried in the slew of things we have to do every day. We can get caught up in grading, planning, and organizing. Our to-do list expands exponentially, and the idea of getting through the end of the unit, let alone designing a unit that inspires the engagement we seek, seems impossible.

The question then becomes, how do we actually ensure that teachers in the modern era will ignite the flame that inspires a student to become an innovator, idea maker, and leader? How do we create the experiences our students need to reach this goal in the midst of our chaotic lives?

Imagine a classroom that consistently taught the whole student in an undeniably engaging way. What would it look like? We bet that it would have some or all of these features:

- Learning experiences that feel authentically relevant
- Acknowledgement of each student as a traveler on an individually tailored learning path

- Deep connections with mentors that shape deep engagement with learning
- Opportunities to learn not only the content of a subject but the application and use of the content
- Practice in authentic situations that show students how to interact with other humans in the real world
- Integration of essential skills outside of content-specific standards

Sounds like a pretty awesome place to learn and grow! So why are these classrooms in the minority?

———

Tiff: I confess to having been sadly surprised when I had my first field experience as an undergraduate education major. I probably shouldn't have been, having gone through thirteen years of K–12 education myself, but I was.

I was taken aback by the classroom I saw, which my professors had chosen as an engaging, inspiring first step in my journey to be an educator. Upon walking in to that first day of my field experience (one of ten weekly visits for the semester), I was excited and eager to talk with students, help them understand content, and be a part of shaping their learning.

What I quickly discovered, however, was that the day-to-day life of a student in school is, quite frankly, boring.

I remember being bored in school, but I always chalked it up to me just being me. I was a spacey child, always reading a book under my desk and rushing through a worksheet so I could just be done and turn it in. I vividly remember my mother making me rewrite my homework because there was no way any human on the face of the planet could possibly understand the words I had scrawled across the page.

As I sat as a silent observer in the back of the room, I recognized that same boredom on almost every child's face. And who could blame them? Their world consisted of worksheets, lessons, practices, quizzes, and tests. Why would they love to see and be a part of the beauty of math when the math they did every day was dull? How could they understand the mystery and complexity of human language when the stories they read held no meaning for them?

———

Chances are, you were bored at some point in your K–12 education. Perhaps not as bored as Tiffany (who, she will readily admit, has the attention span of a squirrel), but bored nonetheless with the learning that you were doing. Your teachers' least favorite question in class was probably, "When are we ever going to use this?" Maybe, as a teacher today, you are unsure how you could answer that question for your own students besides to say, "You will need it for next year" or "If you choose to take chemistry in high school, they will go more deeply into this."

The world around us changes quickly, and those of us in education know that the world of teaching and learning is trying to keep up and stay relevant. New initiatives pop up every year (or multiple times a year), begging us to take up a new cause or examine some new data. Make learning relevant but stick to the standards. Use the curriculum with fidelity, but make sure to personalize learning for our students.

The elephant in the room each day is the question "How will one initiative connect to another?" Furthermore, how will we blend all of these research-based ideas into one another and into the work we did with the previous initiative? How often do we have to start over and reinvent the wheel because we can't seem to connect what we are supposed to be doing in the classroom with what is really important for our students and the world? How do we stitch all these ideas together and use them to engage our students in the ways we know are possible but just can't figure out how to do?

You aren't alone if you feel overwhelmed by all these questions. Maybe you aren't sure how you can tackle one question, let alone that big long list. A good place to start is by reflecting on who you are as an educator and what unique qualities and skills you possess.

ENGAGEMENT YOUR WAY

Right now, the progressive education world is focused on engagement. Let's be honest: You can't spend more than a minute or two on Instagram, Twitter, Facebook, or Pinterest without finding an eye-catching image of a seemingly outstanding educator who must own five Cricut paper cutters and has discovered a way to fit twelve extra work hours into their days. To top it off, these educators are masters at positioning their work in an Instagram-ready photoshoot. What will they think of next?

We love these teachers! (Especially the ones who share ready-for-the-classroom tools!) However, your growth as an educator has to be personal. It has to apply to your life and your students' lives, not your Instagram feed. You don't have to replicate what that amazing Instagram teacher or blogger did to transform your students' classroom experiences.

When people make the choice to change, they always seem to change in the same way they've seen others change. You hear about your friend signing up for a yoga class to start getting toned, so you think, *Gosh, I need to start doing that! I need to go to yoga and get toned! It's working for Michelle, so it's gotta work for me too!*

We see this same phenomenon happen in education. Think about that one teacher in your school who is just absolutely rocking it with songs to teach content or the other teacher who is doing awesome hands-on learning activities with beautifully colored, exquisitely designed paper manipulatives (which you know took hours to cut out). Somehow they are also doing classroom transformations once a week!

What do you do? You start blasting music in your classroom, you start buying neon paper using your own pocket money, and you teach your students songs to learn your content. You try to do it all!

Rae: Early on, my teaching career was quite a learning experience. I took up this sixth-grade math position, and from deep within my core, I wholeheartedly believed I was going to change the world and ski right on through the year, leaving a wake of blissfully happy, engaged, and more intelligent students behind me.

As the year went on, however, I became more confident my year would look more like drowning than water-skiing.

Unsure of where to begin, I returned to the traditional method of how I was taught as a student. I taught a lesson, students practiced, it repeated for three weeks, and then I'd administer a unit test. I would then begin the process over again.

Perhaps I shouldn't have been, but I was surprised when my students did not beat down my door, excited to learn in class each day. I searched and searched for innovative strategies to engage my students with the classroom content. I read teaching books, searched online, and even asked my (very small at the time) personal learning network (PLN) for support.

Everyone was so helpful! Teachers across the country shared resources for teaching specific content, shared their own educational journeys for motivation, and presented me with lists of "games" to engage students. I even had an incredible teacher, Mrs. Hinchie, send me a pack of neon Astrobright paper.

Let me tell you, I was so excited! I tried them all! I was not only eager to learn, but I didn't want to take it slow. I wanted the engagement now!

We aren't going to lie; bright neon paper is really fun. Discovering a resource such as Teachers Pay Teachers can feel like your first sip of hot cocoa—warm, soothing, welcoming. It can feel like the morning of your birthday as a child, when you woke up to presents on the table waiting to be opened. Having a colleague make copies of every math project they've ever used and ceremonially passing it along to you. Reading that first education book that really caught your imagination and inspired you, made you feel like you were a superhero of education, ready to save the day for students everywhere!

Perhaps, then, you have also felt the sharp sting of disappointment when things didn't exactly go as smoothly as you imagined they would.

————————

Rae: *After weeks of neon paper and content games, I started to ask myself some important questions:*

Why was I now working double the number of hours?

Why was I spending so much time on the look of my lesson rather than the purpose?

Why was the new game and brightly colored paper not turning my room into one of the classrooms I had seen on Instagram and Twitter?

I literally had this vision in my mind when I first started implementing these new ideas: Students jumping into the air (in slow motion, of course) eager to learn and celebrating their success. Parents cheering on their students and the magic we were creating through our learning. In my dream, even the news reporters would come to report on what fun school had become. (Sounds like a Hallmark Movie, right?)

Now, don't get me wrong, of course the neon paper added to the eye-appealing thrill of the day. And sure, the "Heads Up" game for students practicing vocabulary was something we all got a good giggle out of . . . but when the games get old or when the cost of neon paper puts too much stress on my bank account, then what?

————————

For two weeks, your trial of incorporating loud music and dance routines is great, but inside it's killing you! You hate loud pop music because it hurts your ears. You don't have the money to keep purchasing paper because you and your family are scraping by, living on a teacher's salary.

Hmm, neon paper or dinner on Tuesday? (I know, it's a tough decision.)

To top it all off, you can barely carry a tune, much less write a purposefully catchy melody for your students. And the real downer is that despite all of your best efforts, it just doesn't seem to be making that big of a difference in your students' engagement levels or interest, and it hasn't really impacted their achievement, either.

You feel like you have failed. After all, what's the alternative? If you don't choose to fashion your teaching after that Instagram-worthy classroom, you are clearly a bad teacher.

Guess what? You're not a bad teacher. This isn't about them, and it isn't about what they do. It's about what you do to reach your students. This is your personal growth journey, your very own educational teaching journey, and it has to fit who you are.

The problem with all the stuff we see on Pinterest and Instagram, and whatever other social media platform pops up down the road, is that none of the posts truly address the most important piece of what will work in your classroom: you and your students.

The idea of copying something that works for someone else is flawed from the start. You need to take the time to reflect on who you are and what your students need. Find your own personal flavor of awesomeness that works.

Take a few minutes and jot down some answers to the following questions or, at the bare minimum, pause long enough to really put some mental energy into reflecting on who you are, what your personal strengths are, and what your students need:

- When are you happiest?
- What is the best lesson or unit you have ever taught? Why?
- What has been your favorite learning experience from your life? Why?
- Do you prefer a bustling, energetic classroom or a calm, reflective classroom? Why?
- What kind of students do you work with? What is their developmental stage? A five-year-old is going to be very different from an eighteen-year-old. Consider how they are similar to or different from each other and also compared with yourself.

Now keep this picture in your mind, keep your notebook close, and consider the following strategies as you imagine what your version of the most engaging learning ever might look like.

A BUFFET OF ENGAGEMENT AWESOMENESS

There are dozens (hundreds?) of engagement strategies that we can try in our classrooms. Song and dance! Room transformations and themed units! The options seem endless (and often overwhelming). Where do you start?

Just like a buffet restaurant, you always need to do one loop of the room to observe all the options before you start filling your plate with the tastiest combination of foods best suited to your tastes. Let's take a little tour of what the engagement buffet might look like:

Let's get personal: Personalized learning helps each student learn content they are interested in that is relevant to the standards and explored at their own pace and in their own way.

Game on: Whether you incorporate games for learning or turn your entire unit or year into an immersive, gamified adventure that supports the themes and goals of your class, dipping into students' drive for challenge, competition, and cooperation can have a big impact on engagement!

Beyond the four walls: Relevance and collaboration are the keys here. Show students the purpose and the reasons behind what they're learning through real community connections.

Get out of the way: Loosen the reins and let them lead!

This list doesn't even come close to all the strategies you have available to make learning more engaging for students, but it is a great starting point for finding what approach fits who you are and works with your needs as well as those of your students. We could spend the next pages discussing each one and outlining ideas for using them in your classroom, but instead let's think about each strategy through the lens of the Teach Better mindset.

Remember, teaching better isn't about perfection. It isn't about being better than the teacher down the hall. There is no need to do a better song and dance than the other teachers in your building or to have a better room transformation than the one you saw on Instagram. It is about being better than what you were yesterday and always striving to be better tomorrow than today. Continuous growth, right?

This means that whatever strategy we choose must be seen from this perspective. What does "Getting out of the way" better mean? How do we "Game on" better?

Let's Get Personal

How cool would it be if every human were able to spend their lives learning what interested them in ways that worked best for them and if they understood what they needed to achieve the learning they desired?

The simple fact is, people just don't work that way. A handful of children will develop a deep interest in a particular subject and absorb as much information as they can from as many sources as possible in their quests for knowledge, but many people never achieve that kind of self-directed learning. So what do we do?

Many efforts toward personalized learning center around choice and voice. Allow students to have choice in the work they do and how they learn it, then encourage them to voice their understanding in a way that works best for them. Choice boards left and right. Tiered learning opportunities here and there. Genius hour everywhere!

Sounds great, right? Well, it doesn't always work out quite that way.

————

Tiff: *A while back, one of my colleagues and I were working on some curriculum design, and I mentioned that I was considering implementing a genius hour model in my classroom. After a longer-than-normal pause, she relayed a story of her own daughter's experience.*

Apparently the mere mention of "genius hour" elicited immediate eye rolls, sighs, and an irritated rant. "I hate genius hour!" paired with "Ugh!" followed by a thorough explanation of everything wrong with it.

I was shocked! I thought students loved genius hour and the freedom it provided to explore what was interesting to them. Turns out, this isn't always the case.

My colleague's daughter experienced her first genius hour as a fourth grader. Initially, she was thrilled! This girl loves learning so much, she soaks up hours of Khan Academy just for fun. She loves to read and think and debate big ideas. She has strong opinions on everything from politics to environmental issues to sociology, and exploring and learning about these things is often self-directed.

Unfortunately, genius hour was an incredible source of stress and frustration for her. Choosing just one topic that interested her out of a thousand different ideas was not just tough; it was crushing. Finally choosing a topic she deemed "good enough," she started her planning and research only to be faced with requirements of "thick" questions and "un-googleable" questions.

What had started as a great opportunity for exploration and learning became ridden with requirements and restrictions that made it feel like anything but gloriously personalized experiences. The promise of being able to learn what she wanted to learn turned into just another project to do and another checklist to complete. It left her with an intense resistance to future "voice and choice" learning opportunities.

————

Don't get us wrong, genius hour can be amazing and well worth the effort, and there are plenty of students who find a lot of value in that experience even if my friend's daughter hated it. But promising free rein to explore something a student is interested in and then shackling them with a slew of requirements is a recipe for bitterness and frustration.

What about choice boards? You spend your time crafting a choice board with a variety of options for students, some challenging and others more straightforward. You try to have artistic options, research options, and performance options so there is something that appeals to everyone.

Then you hand them out and boom! Awesomeness ensues. Or does it? Maybe the following situations sound familiar:

Student A should choose the more challenging tasks because she is ready for that level of difficulty; however, she is pretty savvy and has figured out that the more challenging choices would take a lot of mental effort, so she chooses the three most straightforward options. It takes her two class periods to finish, and the work she turns in is not even close to what she is capable of.

Student B is right on grade level and chooses three tasks of varying difficulty. Great! Throughout the week of classes, he works hard, and it is clear that he has reinforced his understanding through his work.

Student C is struggling with the content. He is not a big fan of artistic choices and wouldn't be caught dead performing something that demonstrated his understanding. He chooses the research-based option even though it is the most challenging, and he struggles the whole week. Unfortunately, he doesn't further his understanding of the content, because he spends so much time frustrated, trying to understand what he needs to do.

If our classes were made up entirely of Student Bs, we would be fine. Choice boards would work well. But, as you know, they are not.

So what do we do? Let's take a step back and consider the fundamental purpose of personalization: giving each student the learning experiences best suited to their needs, interests, and abilities at that moment so they are able and want to engage with the content fully. If we think about it, choice boards and genius hour miss this mark! They are valiant attempts at this goal, but they really only scratch the surface.

What if, instead, we considered a radical shift in how we think about the students in our classrooms? What if we were able to strike a balance between guiding our students through the content enough that they do not flounder in the endless sea of options, while also fostering the independence and self-direction that will serve them well in the future?

This was the same predicament that Chad experienced before developing his own self-paced framework to try and personalize the learning experience.

––––––––––

Chad: *Through trial and error, providing pure choice and freedom never seemed to work or connect for me, and giving rigid, non-flexible instruction had its obvious flaws. It was the middle ground where the most success was found. By creating structured systems and routines and providing a clear learning path for students in the form of mastery Grids, I was able to step back and let my students lead our classroom.*

While the mastery Grids laid out the learning path for my students, they had options on how to show mastery, and it was easily adjustable "on the fly."

This provided the key to success and personalization that was both empowering and effective for learners. As students began working at their own paces and proving their mastery, I realized that student-centered classrooms and personalization didn't mean "no control." They meant strategic control. By controlling the environment with curriculum, structure, and routine, student freedom was able to flourish, which allowed true personalization to occur.

––––––––––

When you provide your students with an environment that offers structured choice and the freedom to learn the way that best suits each individual, something truly amazing happens. Students own it! Students begin to feel the control you've provided them, and they take on the responsibility of their learning journey. *When you see a student that truly owns his or her learning, it is simply awesome.*

––––––––––

Jeff: *Chad and I had the opportunity to visit Rae's class shortly after we connected through Twitter. Let me just tell you, Rae's class is awesome. I remember walking into the room during a transition as the music playing changed from an upbeat song to instrumental light music. I smelled a scented candle in the corner; it made the room feel (and smell) warm and inviting. Even with all these calming elements, there was a palpable buzz as each student was fully engaged in their own personalized learning activities. Each student was being met where they were and working on what they needed at that time.*

It's pretty cool to witness so many different things going on at the same time, and even more so to see it happening with no disruptions, no chaos, and no headaches for the teacher.

Within seconds of walking into Rae's classroom, we knew we were going to witness awesomeness. And we didn't have to wait long.

Shortly after we arrived, a student approached Rae to ask how she was going to accomplish a piece of her project. Here's how the conversation played out:

Student: Mrs. Hughart, can I create a video to complete this assignment?

Rae: I don't know. What do you think?

That's it! Seriously. That was the entire conversation, and the student went right back to work.

You see, as soon as Rae replied, this student remembered something: She was in control of her learning, not Rae. Her face went from "I'm not sure if I'm allowed to do this" to "Oh, that's right! I own this!"

———

Here was a young girl, a sixth grader, fully in control of her education. Rae had provided her with everything she needed to succeed. More importantly, Rae had provided the student with an environment and a culture that instilled ownership, confidence, opportunity for risk, and the opportunity for success in her.

Making learning personal is a strategy that increases engagement and works really well for a lot of teachers, but maybe it isn't something that you feel comfortable tackling right now. Maybe you tried to personalize and ran into countless obstacles. That doesn't mean you have to give up on the idea forever, but maybe a different strategy would be a good thing to try.

Game on

Gamification and game-based learning! Competition and cooperation! Points and leveling up! Sounds like fun, right?

———

Tiff: A few summers back, I read Michael Matera's book Explore Like a Pirate, *and I dove in headfirst to a yearlong gamification adventure! My students became wizards and mages and warriors, and I greeted them on the first day of school in a long wizard cloak and carrying a staff.*

It. Was. Awesome.

The first few weeks of class, they were so into it that all the learning we did came with ease. Earning experience points for learning content led to learning new spells. New spells led to more powerful attacks against the big boss. Playing a game of Kahoot a few weeks in, it was obvious that my students knew the content like the back of their hand. We were on fire!

And then we weren't.

Students started losing interest in experience points and challenges. I forgot to keep track of how many hit points the big boss still had. And the double-digit multiplication unit we'd just started wasn't going well.

What went wrong? That intense engagement Tiffany was looking for seemed to vanish into thin air, and she was left at square one. Sure, kids still liked playing class Jeopardy, but mostly so they could be called the winner, not so they could review the content they had learned.

Tiff: *Back to the drawing board. (My drawing board sure does get a lot of use.) Why weren't students interested anymore? Why was it becoming so difficult to manage? How could we have just played a review game, and suddenly they didn't remember anything?*

I whipped out the Breakout EDU kit and spent hours building an adventure. Maybe that would work? Sure. For a day.

As I sat there after school picking up the pieces of the day's game, it hit me: None of this matters. None of it

INTERESTED IN GAMIFICATION?

Explore Like a Pirate author, Michael Matera, breaks it down step by step. Find the book and more resources at teachbetter.com/BookResources.

has meaning or relevance to what we are learning or to my students' lives. Just like a new toy from their birthday party, the game had lost its luster, and the students weren't into it anymore.

Creating an awesome gamification adventure and designing educational games for your students can take hours (and days and weeks) of planning time, but if you forget to make it matter for your students, it will be hours of work with little effect on learning.

Engagement comes from meaning and relevance. Tiffany's awesome wizarding magical adventure was cool but completely irrelevant!

Tiff: Third time's the charm, right? This time the game took on new meaning. Yes, I still donned the wizard cape and held my staff, but this time the mission I sent my students on to earn points connected the content to the game. We were stampeding the castle of our mortal enemy: the evil wizard Darth Shackleton. Students worked in teams to calculate the supplies needed, shop around, bargain with different innkeepers to find the best price based on the amount of money they were able to scrape together, then predict the success of their mission based on predictions of the mystical oracle (a six-sided die).

Probability, multiplication, decimals? Check! Creating and solving equations? Check! Developing communication and collaboration skills? Check!

The best part? There were no worksheets with dozens of practice problems. No online practice games. There was nothing that felt like a regular class assignment. They discovered strategies for multi-digit multiplication based on their need to determine supply cost. The game was the learning, and the learning was the game.

Cloaking practice problems and regular lessons in isolated puzzles or games can be temporarily engaging, but it does little to build engagement for longer than a day or two. Marrying the game to the learning is what makes the "Game on" strategy engage better. Send your students on a journey. Give them missions and goals. Let them explore and invent strategies to complete their missions, and they will learn the content you need them to along the way!

Beyond the Four Walls

Imagine a world where the local coffee shop invested in the success of the community's youth, whom they serve. Where an insurance company's CEO felt responsibility for the success of a learner. Where those walking the streets of our town began to take ownership of supporting classrooms financially, emotionally, and academically. Imagine a time when teachers adjusted the "What do you want to be when you grow up?" question to "What problems do you want to solve?" or "What impact would that have on the current system?" or "What effects would that investment carry long term?"

Educational philosopher John Dewey argued that content had little meaning if not connected to its real-world application outside of the school system. To ensure this is at the forefront of your instruction, you must challenge lessons to encompass more than an isolated, tunnel-vision view but actively choose to involve others in student learning. Connecting your classroom to the community not only engages your students with the world around you but also connects the world around them to the schools. Win–win!

If you are an educator already organizing career days to bring community members to schools, having students create holiday cards for a local nursing home, and hosting the occasional guest speaker in the classroom, kudos to you. We recognize you for the work you have done, and because we are who we are, we challenge you to take it further. Use the power of the world beyond your four walls to engage your students better.

It is not enough to just foster a connection in the spring during a career expo or plan an epic review for your Friday class. Why not? Well . . . what about Wednesday? Or Thursday? Or all those days in the fall?

There is danger in this approach to connecting with the community. If our approach to engagement and bringing purpose into the classroom is only obtainable in isolated instances, what happens when our students miss it? What if the one time a week you cover a life-changing topic is the same day your student is distracted with worry? What if several have the flu? What if the spring career expo falls on the same day a student has a doctor's appointment?

No more what-ifs! We need great instruction not just on fun Fridays but also Mondays, Tuesdays, Wednesdays, and Thursdays. Students don't need a once-in-a-lifetime, life-changing, interdisciplinary unit in October. They need your very best in September, November, December . . . . You get the picture, right?

One really awesome day, event, or lesson followed by dull, boring ones for the next six weeks won't cut it. It is possible to take advantage of the connections just waiting to happen all around you, to bring meaning to your lessons every day, every week, all year long.

Consider for a moment a traditional model for teaching a math lesson. Start with the basics, build on the skills one by one, and conclude with those ever-challenging word problems. But what if we switched that up a bit? What if your students were caught living in the word problem and unable to find success without your content's help? What would happen if your students actively lived in the "why" behind your learning before even beginning a lesson? They would be actively engaged in the solution.

Sounds great, right? The challenge we are faced with is, how on Earth do we make this type of engagement manageable?

––––––––––

Rae: During my first few years in education, I found myself incredibly frustrated that every day seemed to present a new challenge in terms of engaging students.

How was I going to engage them? What tricks did I have up my sleeves? Forcing a smile, presenting unbridled enthusiasm, and doing a song-and-dance routine every single day just isn't going to happen on those mornings when you are falling apart and just can't do it anymore.

How do you ensure a purposeful lesson with the highest possible engagement occurs on those days?

To be honest, I searched for solutions to this problem for a long time. Frustrated by only finding pieces and parts of ideas without a unifying structure that made them all work, I decided I would just design my own system.

I chose to immerse my students every day of the year in themed mock internships sponsored by local businesses. As we worked within these internships, we emphasized the value the content had in our own lives. And with the use of local businesses, we achieved three things:

1. *Students could walk outside and see our classroom in action.*
2. *Students finally felt like they were actually a part of something bigger than themselves.*
3. *We finally built stakeholders in my students extending outside the walls of our classroom, outside the walls of our students' homes, and into the community— stakeholders who had a reason to begin investing in the students in our schools.*

———

Through career-themed units focusing on future professional paths, transformative classroom environments, and strong community support, each unit concludes with a community outreach challenge, disbursing student learning back into the community. And the impact on Rae's students' lives was enormous.

———

Rae: *You know those moments you sometimes have when everything comes together, perhaps with a shining spotlight and dramatic background music, and suddenly you achieve clarity and understanding? After my own learning struggles, after getting into my dream college, after graduating from that college, and after beginning my career in education, I had my moment.*

One year in November, as I was crawling toward Thanksgiving break, I opened my inbox to a whole slew of emails. Notes about students on the cross-country team leaving early for a meet, a PE class letting students out late, a parent email or two questioning the dates for Thanksgiving break due to family vacations, and one more with an email address I didn't recognize.

The subject, all in lowercase, said, "hi ms ford."

My maiden name was Ford, and I had only served two years of my teaching career using this name before I married my husband. Now, after having spent most of my career as Mrs. Hughart, any email acknowledging me as a Ms. Ford could only be from a very special group of students whom I was able to spend time with early in my career. A very special group of students who would always have a sacred place in my heart.

Curious, I clicked open the email. Inside was a two-paragraph note. I barely read the beginning and quickly skimmed down to the end. The email concluded with "hope all is well, jessica."

Jessica was a student who had sat quietly in class. She rarely had made eye contact and took almost the whole school year to warm up to me. Although I remember her spending most of her time alone, she'd had one good friend I occasionally saw her laughing with.

I always worried about her.

Jessica's short email began with her asking how I was and whether I was still teaching. She explained she'd tracked down my new email from an old colleague and wanted to reach out to tell me about her life since we had last spoken. She was a junior in high school and had just applied to a few local colleges. She told me that her dream since sixth grade was to become an architect after she experienced one of my math-themed internships with an architecture focus.

She remembered interacting with numerous architects from the immediate community as well as some from Chicago. She learned about the profession and applied what these connections told her to the work she did in class.

The unit concluded with an architecture tour in the city of Chicago and a visit to the Illinois Holocaust Museum. It was Jessica's first trip to a large city.

"No one ever talked to me about college because college is not something we do in my family. But I have to go, because I learned I have a dream.—Jessica."

―――――――

No matter your dream as an educator, the impact of connecting content to your students' immediate world and their futures can spark a dream within someone else. You cannot make that type of impact with an engaging review game on a Monday or colorful classroom décor on a Friday. For this, you need purpose that envelops the student in the "why" each and every moment of learning. That is how the purpose of the learning sticks. That is how we transform learning classroom content beyond the four walls of the classroom.

Remember, the content we teach is not the goal. The content is the tool we use to reach the goal of developing human beings intimately connected to, interested in, and engaged with the world around them, eager to enhance it with their own special skills.

————————

Rae: When I began leading my classroom in this way, I went through a slew of powerful, themed internship units with a smattering of ineffective ones. Making this process manageable became an enormous focus. Yes, the system was relatively successful in my classroom, but to make a real impact, I couldn't just keep guessing at what each unit would look like.

In typical teacher fashion, I laid out all the essentials.

Starting with the standards, I used the backward design to ensure each element of my curriculum led to mastering the standard expectation. I then evaluated the content's purpose to best identify an internship theme that would both encompass the content's "why" and my students' interests. Now it was time to reach out to sponsors! Last but not least, each unit would include three key pieces:

1. *Intro Day—The Introduction Day will be the first element of the unit your students will experience; therefore, let's make it magical. The purpose behind this is to focus on how you will hook your student. How will you earn your students' buy-in?*
2. *Big Review Day—The Big Review Day will be the last element of the unit your students will experience before their final assessment. The purpose behind this is to focus on how your students can practice their learning in a real-world situation.*
3. *Community Outreach—There are two types of out-reach activities to consider for your students. One allows your community to enter into your classroom (Inward) and the other allows your students to share their learning with the community (Outward). While you do not need to organize both types of outreach opportunities within every unit, outreach activities can bring incredible value to your students' learning, DOK, and community support. They just worked to master this content—go share it with the world!*

WHAT'S TEACH FURTHER?

Learn more about the Teach Further Model and how to immerse your students in themed internships at teachbetter.com/BookResources.

When you choose to go beyond the four walls of your classroom, your students have the opportunity to become active participants in and influencers of the real world.

Get out of Their Way

Don't steal their ice cream. That might sound a little odd, but think about a common scenario that happens in classrooms around the world. You have just introduced a new unit about the solar system. You showed an engaging video that piqued students' curiosity and posed some interesting questions that will guide them in their learning during the unit. Imagine the following scenario:

After twenty minutes of discussion and exploration, you realize it is time to move on to the vocabulary lesson you had planned. If you don't get to it, students won't be able to do the homework you assigned. Four or five students raise their hands. One student seems to be exploding out of his skin with excitement to share another piece of information he knows about the solar system. Of course, he has already shared four or five obscure facts about Saturn and attempted to teach us all the history of manned space missions. You hurriedly wave at him to put his hand down and tell the students, "We don't have time for any more questions or comments. We need to move on now!"

You have just stolen their ice cream. A delicious ice cream cone is one of the best parts of a summer day, just like an inquisitive exploration based on interests is one of the best parts of learning. What an awesome moment of inquiry and engagement you just missed! What a chance to let students learn from each other and explore ideas together you have just wasted! Let's consider for a moment what would happen if you went a different route.

The student who is so excited to share his knowledge is allowed to speak. His enthusiasm for the subject brings other students into the world of space exploration. You realize, as the student tells the class about how Pluto used to be a planet, then wasn't, that they have just covered one of your standards about the various objects in the solar system.

The discussion of dwarf planets and planets takes up most of the class period as students ask about other dwarf planets and have a spontaneous student-led moment of silence for the planet that was demoted. At the end of class, you realize that you do not have time for that vocabulary activity you wanted to get to, but decide that you can assign them a Quizlet vocabulary list for homework instead of what you had originally planned. Will this conversation set you back a bit in your pacing? Maybe. But you can probably make up some of that time when you were planning on discussing dwarf planets anyway.

When we get out of our students' way, we accomplish multiple goals: increased student engagement because they have more control and more input into what they learn and when, and increased interest as students explore and discuss aspects of the content that pique their curiosity. The most awesome part of learning is discovery, wonder, and questioning. It is like the ice cream you got after an especially tough basketball game or the best part of a birthday party—ice cream cake!

Consider channeling your students' interest and excitement through facilitated class discussions. Let student interests guide the conversation while you perform mental acrobatics on a second's notice to make sure you are still on topic enough to teach what you need to teach. Students studying ecology want to bring in a cool bug they found at home? Let them! A student wants to show you the remote-control car they have during a unit on energy? Let them! Find ways to channel their interest that honor their exploration and move learning forward.

Choose Your Own Path

The four strategies explored here are not by any means the only ways to engage students! Maybe you are contemplating trying one of them, or perhaps you have your own ideas that you want to try. Go for it! Whatever you choose to explore, be sure that you continuously reflect, revise, and tweak your approach. Real success and transformative learning experiences with any of these engagement strategies won't happen with a half-done, sort-of isolated experience. Sure, those are great ways to start, but, like Tiffany's gamification experience and Rae's experiences connecting with the community, the magic really happened when they committed to reflection and revision in their efforts.

An idea is a good start. Beginning to use the idea takes us to the next step. But a steady commitment to continuous improvement? That's how we help our students soar and engage better.

STORIES FROM THE TEACH BETTER COMMUNITY

> GO *POKÉMON!* HUNTING: ADAM PETERSON (@TEACHERSLEARN2)
Adam Peterson Education (adampetersoneducation.com)

My most proud moment as a teacher was hearing parents say, "My son can't wait to go back to school!" or "My daughter doesn't like weekends because she misses your classroom so much!" I'm not going to lie; I lived for compliments like that! No, no, no . . . it wasn't because it boosted my ego as a teacher. I never actually that it was specifically because of me at all. I believe those feelings from my students were fueled by one factor found on a daily basis in my classroom: ENGAGEMENT!

You see, I learned from an early stage in my teaching career that it isn't all about "what" we teach but more about "how" we teach it. I studied my curriculum and standards and realized that nowhere in the stuff I had to teach did it ever tell me how I had to teach it! I used that revelation to create the most engaging, fun, and exciting classroom I possibly could. I picked up my guitar and put down my teacher manuals. I got off my stool and turned on my dance moves. I taught less to my kiddos and taught more with them. I began seeing my students more engaged when I started involving them more in the classroom. I sought out their interests and passions and used those to create a classroom environment that was impossible to be unengaged in.

Am I a perfect teacher? NO! Have there been times when my methods haven't worked? Yes, of course! But I didn't let failures or fear stand in my way. My favorite example of this happened in the fall of 2017. I had a student who was obsessed with *Pokémon*! He didn't care that I was dancing around the classroom or that I played the guitar and sang silly songs. He was not engaged in any of my lessons, and I was worried that I had a student in my class who already didn't love school.

So I spent a weekend learning everything I could about *Pokémon*. I used our usual unit on "Getting to Know the School" but turned it into a giant week-long game of *Pokémon* hunting! We spent the week doing crafts, playing games, learning math, and reading books all while learning about *Pokémon*! On Friday I dressed up as Ash Ketchum, distributed *Pokémon* characters to teachers around the building, hid clues, and then we spent the morning hunting *Pokémon* while learning the names and locations of important teachers in our building.

Guess what? That student was engaged. He had the time of his life. And he loved coming to school. Not to mention the other kids had a blast as well! You see, creating engaging environments is as simple as tapping into the passions of your students, using your knowledge of your curriculum and standards, and blending it all in a way that works for you and your students!

CHAPTER 5
FAIL BETTER

"FAILURE IS NOT THE END. IN FACT, IT IS THE BEGINNING OF A BEAUTIFUL JOURNEY,"

–JADE YOUSSEF

The four of us are intimately familiar with failure. I'd say we each fail on a daily basis, if not dozens of times each day; in fact, writing this book has been a series of failures percolated by the occasional bright ray of clarity. We fail in our classrooms, we fail in book writing, we fail in finding where we put a student's paper to grade or remembering to send that important email to a conference we are supposed to present at.

––––––––

Rae: Working on this chapter today seems humorous because, well, I failed today. I failed five times today. I failed first period, fourth period, fifth period, sixth period, and eighth period. But who's counting, right?

I arrived at school today two hours before the initial school bell. I am a morning person with a to-do list longer than my commute. I skipped the dogs' long morning walk and headed to school bright and early. (Or dark and early for those of you who know the sun is never up early enough when you need to have a productive morning work session.)

Driving to work, I watched the sun rise as I traveled down empty streets with an endless list of tasks on my mind. Needless to say, when I finally turned into my typical parking spot, I knew exactly what I intended to cover first. As I began working, the task of checking my email was number five on the list. When I got to my inbox (about forty-five minutes before the first bell), I noticed a message from my student teacher saying she was ill and would not make it to school that day.

"Ugh." I sighed, trying to remember the topic of her mini lesson and realizing I'd needed to find a way to prepare a similar lesson in her absence. Absolute value and opposites, here we go!

After brainstorming for a while, I had a great plan! My idea was interactive, easily relatable, had an epic student hook, and even linked to our math-themed internship by allowing students to travel to a new country we had not yet studied. I was so proud of this idea, I recorded multiple Instagram stories sharing our class plan for the day, breaking down each moment of the class hour to share with other teachers interested in new ideas.

First period—The lesson was underway! I was excited and shared my eager-to-learn demeanor with my hour-one students. It was a bit long (about fourteen minutes), but students seemed content with the information. As the formative assessments continued to roll in throughout the class hour, what did they consistently get wrong? Absolute value and opposites! I have to hit that harder, I thought, jotting down small adjustments I intended to make to the lesson.

Then fourth period arrived. With my adjustments, I got my students back on their personalized learning pathway after a sixteen-minute mini lesson. Still, as formative assessments continued, students continued to incorrectly answer questions related to absolute value. Something was not working.

I continued in this pattern for three other class periods. Reflection. Adjustment. Repeat; nevertheless, even by the last class period of the day, a minority group were considered absolute value and opposite masters.

Arriving home frustrated, I began working on my other to-do list tasks and saw that adding to this chapter—all about failure—was at the top of the list.

There are so many meaningful reflection opportunities we as educators must choose to take for both the betterment of our students and the betterment of ourselves. And while each day seems like a constant hike from a good lesson to a great lesson or a surprising pitfall from a good lesson to a fall, we must continue to strive to fail forward. Remember, any day can be an opportunity to do it better next time. Guess what I am teaching again tomorrow?

In this chapter, we are going to talk a lot about student failure and how you as an educator can use that failure as a launching point to deeper learning, a critical component of appropriately challenging education.

Before we can start that conversation, we have to have this one first:

You will fail.

Educators around the world are getting pretty good at recognizing that struggle is an important piece of the learning puzzle: growth mindset, failing forward, and shifting the conversation from "I can't" to "I can't . . . yet" are commonplace in classrooms and school buildings. We push every day to share this with our students and teach them that failure is part of their journey because we know how important it is for them to have that "fail forward" mindset. The simple truth, though, is that we are not always very good at developing that mindset in ourselves.

We must learn how to fail better.

To fail better is not just accepting that failure is a part of the journey and looking for the lessons learned with each failure. To fail better is to take it one step further. It is about reflecting on the path that has led us to where we are today and using what we see there to push ourselves even further.

Think about your life up to this point right now. We would be willing to bet that the road is littered with failures—big ones, small ones, and life-altering awful ones. When you think back to all of those little mistakes, all of those huge disasters, we want you to consider that every single one of them has led you to where you are today. They have led you to this exact moment.

There is a good chance that you may not be exactly where you want to be in life. But you are here, and you are where you need to be. You are working hard to change the lives of your students and pursuing your own growth and development to create the most amazing education experience for the students who come into your room every day. And that is awesome!

So even though it probably seems like it has been a pretty bumpy road, all of those bumps helped guide you here, to this book, to this decision to Teach Better.

Failures act as road signs even if we don't always see them. They steer us away from things that don't work, mistakes we've made, both big and small. Sometimes we aren't very good at seeing these signs, and sometimes we choose to ignore them, but the fact remains that they were there the whole way here, showing us the path forward.

Remember that time you tried something new in your classroom? Maybe it was a new system or routine, and the students didn't catch on because it was just a little too complicated. Perhaps it was a new approach to inquiry-driven learning that was cool to do but didn't really improve learning. It could have been a new tech tool that you thought was going to skyrocket success and ended up being a distraction and ineffective. At the time, you may have viewed these failures as a case of your students not being able to understand, or a result of the materials and tools you used being subpar, but maybe it was just a sign that you needed to adjust the way you implemented the ideas.

Failures transform us, shaping our minds, our souls, and our abilities to adapt and grow. Every time we fail, we're given the opportunity to learn and grow. These opportunities don't have to come from massive, life-altering failures; they can come from even the smallest mistakes.

Think of all the little failures you've had. At the time, you may have brushed them off as minor, but they are part of your journey here. It could have been that time you locked yourself out of the house but quickly found a way to get back in. It seems like a small, inconsequential mistake, but it tests your adaptability. It challenges your ability to remain calm in a frustrating situation. And it forces you to grow. You probably haven't done it too many times since!

––––––––––

Jeff: *I always say that I have been very fortunate to fail a lot in my life. I typically say it with a smile on my face and from a place of appreciation. I appreciate every failure I've had because they have led me to where I am today. But this doesn't mean I appreciated each of them at the time they occurred. Quite the opposite is true for most of them.*

From a very young age, I had a dream of being a rock star. True, this is not an unusual dream. Lots of people wanted to be a rock star when they were young. But I had a different end game in mind than most. My dream was to become a famous rock star and then start my own record label to help other people chase that same dream.

As I got a bit older and started a couple of bands, I realized how ridiculously hard the first part was. Not that the second was easy by any means, but becoming a rock star? One in a million doesn't even do it justice. I decided to focus on the second part instead.

And so, FTF Records was born.

Over the next five years, I signed three acts to recording contracts and four to management deals. I worked with my artists to help them release albums, tour the country, and chase their dreams. I got to speak at music conferences around the country and in Canada, met some of the coolest people in the world, created a concert promotions company that put on more than 150 shows per year, and held a music business conference in my home state, which welcomed musicians and industry reps from all over the world.

I had an office full of interns, an assistant to help me run the show, and a partner managing the concert promotion division. I was living my dream! I was "JefFTF!"

———————

Jeff knows firsthand the power (and struggle) of failure. He doesn't just go on and on about failure because he has read that it is important; he has felt it. We won't gloss over this situation, because it is far too important for us to trivialize. Some of Jeff's failures broke him.

———————

Jeff: *When my record label went under, I had to tell my artists that I couldn't finish their albums, tell my staff that it was over, and tell my family that I had failed. It was one of the worst moments of my life. For five years I had poured every ounce of blood, sweat, and tears I had into that company and my artists. But it was a bad time in the industry, I had made some mistakes, and it just wasn't working.*

I had to tell my artists that I couldn't help them anymore. I had to tell them, "I failed you."

For five years my wife, Amy, had stood beside me, believing in this crazy dream of mine. She never wavered, she never complained, and she never once suggested I give up. Even when it got bad, she stood strong.

After spending countless hours addressing envelopes to send to management companies and concert promoters, working the merchandise tables at shows, staying up all night to piece together programs for the music conference we put on, and even allowing my artists to practice in our basement when they needed a rehearsal space, she had poured just as much blood, sweat, and tears into that dream as I had, with the added sacrifice of not seeing me for days at a time. And I had failed her.

For five years I had been known as "JefFTF" in the local music scene. I was someone people looked to for advice. I was someone people counted on for help. I was someone. What was I now? I was a failure. I had failed my artists. I had failed my team. I had failed my wife. I had failed my family who had supported me and believed in me the entire time. I was destroyed.

———————

Jeff did not see the lessons learned from that failure (that massive group of failures) until many years later; in fact, he'll be the first to tell you he still learns lessons from those failures every day that he reflects on them.

––––––––

Jeff: *I did my best to hide the depression I had fallen into, mainly by avoiding people and avoiding the topic however I could. I got a job and just went to work and came home, put on a smile, and pretended everything was okay.*

But I was consumed with regret, sadness, and shame. I started to shut people out of my life. I ignored phone calls, avoided going out to events, and lied to anyone who asked me how I was doing.

The funny thing is, looking back now, the way I handled that initial failure actually led me to make more mistakes and fail even worse at getting over it. It's just that those lessons were the least of my worries at the time. Thinking back, though, I wonder if I could have come out of that slump sooner if I had had the same outlook on failure as I do today, and if I had reflected and seen those lessons right away.

––––––––

That's the thing about failing better—it's a process. You most likely won't immediately see the lesson in every failure. It might take you years to be able to see what went wrong, how you could have been better, and how to avoid the same in the future. Sometimes it will take someone else reflecting with you to see the lesson (or lessons) you've missed.

Here is what we would like you to do to help find and celebrate the failures in your journey as a teacher. Think back to a time when it all fell apart. You had an awful evaluation. A parent screamed at you over the phone (or in person). Students started throwing pencils, paper, and lab equipment across the room despite your repeated insistence that they stop. (Yes, that actually happened to Tiffany. It was a low point for sure.)

Don't just read past that paragraph and move on. Really take the time right now to stop and identify what you feel has been the biggest moment of failure in your teaching career.

Did you do it? We are serious!

Good job! Sometimes forcing ourselves to take the time needed to reflect is not as easy as it seems. But that reflection is the single most important step toward growth. Maybe that moment you thought of happened ten years ago. Maybe it happened ten minutes ago. It doesn't much matter when it happened. It matters what we do with that failure and where we go from here.

Now that you have that failure in your mind, take some time to ponder why that moment felt so awful. Why did that failure sting so badly? Most importantly, what can it teach you?

Tiff: *I am not perfect.*

I know, I know. That seems impossible, right? (Ha!)

A good portion of this book is all of us confessing our own failures and shortcomings. We have been there! We still make mistakes! And if we aren't comfortable enough to confess our mistakes and failures to you, then we can't very well expect you to confess your failures and mistakes to yourself and grow from them.

So I am going to take you on a journey to one of my most epic failures as a teacher.

When my youngest daughter, Kiya, was born, I had just moved back to Ohio from North Carolina and was between teaching jobs. Eventually, I was able to get a job as a long-term substitute that looked like it had great potential to turn into a full-time position the next year.

Boy oh boy, was I excited! Things had been really tough for the previous few months since our move to Ohio. We were broke, living in my parents' basement (yep, we were those millennials), and my husband was going to school full time while working part time at Arby's bringing home next to nothing.

It was go time! I was ready to knock this one out of the park and show the district that I could create transformative, collaborative, challenging, and inspiring lessons for my students. I needed to make myself indispensable!

After a few months there building relationships, teaching awesome lessons, and basically rocking it out, I began to develop a unit for my gifted enrichment class all about psychology. I wanted to lead them in an exploration of how the human brain works after finding a really interesting psychology book for kids in the office I had inherited. It had dozens of questionnaires, conversation starters, and ideas that I thought would be powerful learning experiences for a conversation about differences, mental health, and the power of self.

Sounds great, right?

My students jumped into the work and were deeply engaged and curious about the topic. Class discussions flourished, and we got into some meaty, tough issues about mental health.

What I failed to consider was the perception of this unit from key stakeholders, most notably parents.

Some parents felt I was discussing inappropriate content and that we were spending our class time "diagnosing" case studies. They felt the material was too mature for their sixth graders and complained (loudly) to administration.

May came around, and I was informed that the district had decided to go in a different direction and would not be offering me a full-time position.

It would be easy in this situation to lash out at parents and administration for not understanding the greater purpose and deeper conversation about how minds work and how mental health affects all of us. It would be easy to live in a bubble of anger and resentment.

––––––––

We aren't going to sugarcoat it: That is exactly what Tiffany did.

––––––––

Tiff: *I crashed. I burned.*

Rather than accept personal responsibility for the content I taught and the way it was received, I blamed everyone in the situation except myself.

I needed that job. My family needed that job.

It wasn't until several years later, after I found a job in another district, that I was able to reflect on that moment as one of personal failure. Not one of other peoples' failures. It was only then that I was finally able to learn from the experience and use it as a launching point toward awesomeness.

It became a part of my routine not to avoid these meaty, important conversations, but to communicate openly and often with parents and administration. I moved forward in my career with a greater sense of the larger world my students existed in and how my own actions in the classroom impacted that world.

––––––––

Let's go back for a minute to that memory you pulled up a few paragraphs ago—the epic failure you experienced as an educator—and look at it through a different lens. What about that situation made it feel so icky? Why did that failure rock you to your core? How did that failure impact your teaching?

If your failure pushed you into a point of retreat, resentment, or anger, we want to encourage you to shift your perspective. In life, there are many things that we cannot control. The one thing we can control? The reactions we have to life's circumstances.

Consider how you reacted to that failure. Did you learn from it in a positive way?

Tiffany Example		
What was my failure?	How did I respond to this failure?	What could/should I have learned?
Not getting a full-time position after a long-term substitute position.	Despair at my family situation.	A great idea is the first step. Implementing it well is the second. Communication is key.
I planned a psychology unit, and parents complained.	Anger and irritation at parents and administration.	Consider your audience (more than your students). Parents are advocates for their students.

So now we want you to take out a piece of paper, your phone, or your computer, and spend a few minutes reflecting on that failure. The format in the table can guide your reflection.

Our failures must become more than just failures. They must show us what we can learn. But we have to be willing to see it. When Tiffany thinks about that moment in her journey, she uses it to push herself forward, to shape the ways in which she works with parents and administration. She actually shares this failure with people all the time. Not only does it help her grow, it is a story that has helped her forge relationships with others going through similar challenges. It has brought her closer to colleagues and administration by pushing to be a better communicator.

How will your failure push you forward? What can you learn from your biggest failures (and all the ones still to come in your future)?

IT ISN'T OUR JOB TO TEACH MATH (OR SCIENCE OR READING OR ART OR . . .)

There is an important truth in education that is often overlooked: We do not teach content. We do not teach the history of the American Revolution or the mechanics of bone and muscle. We do not teach grammar or how to add fractions.

We teach kids.

If we misinterpret our failures as a wall rather than a path, our students struggle even more. Young people have an innate need for recognition, acceptance, and love, and when we see failures (like a low grade on a test or a missing homework assignment) as stopping points for our students, they begin to fear and avoid the very mistakes that will help them grow.

In a traditional classroom, failure represents the end of learning or at least the marker that a goal has not been obtained, a student has not been successful, and the class is moving on without them.

Here is one of the most broken cycles that occur in classrooms:

1. A student takes an assessment.
2. The student fails.
3. It is recorded, and the curriculum or instruction moves on.
4. The student still doesn't understand the content, and now he or she has gaps in knowledge moving into the next unit.
5. The next unit begins, and the student is lost before the end of day one.

And the cycle repeats.

I want you to picture an elementary student who is working on single-digit addition. The class works on the content for a while and then, on a predetermined date, at a predetermined time, they take an end-of-week quiz. The quiz is graded, and the student earns a failing score. When the curriculum and pacing guide say to move on to two-digit addition, how can we reasonably expect that student to suddenly understand? If they can't understand how to add two and two to get four, adding eleven and twelve becomes a herculean task.

You have seen this happen in your class; we are sure of it. The pacing guide says that you need to move on to unit two. Most of the class understands the concept. You, the teacher, feel immense pressure to keep going even when the student simply isn't ready.

That child now feels lost and frustrated and loses confidence in their own ability. This is an all-too-familiar situation for so many of us. As a student, Rae's own brushes with failure almost wrecked her.

———

Rae: *As a student, learning and failure seemed synonymous. Growing up in a northern suburb of Chicago, I had incredible support both at home and in the school I attended. I had a beautiful kitchen table where my parents committed hours of time helping me with homework; nevertheless, regardless of the time spent on homework, learning was a challenge, and every weekday was a reminder of how behind I was compared with my peers.*

My husband, Dan, often proclaims a phrase that perfectly sums up my time in the educational rigmarole: "I am in a perpetual state of winging it." While I can relate to this quote so much more as a teacher continually working to be flexible in my classroom, this directly relates to my time sitting in class as a young student.

I was in a perpetual state of winging it. I remember often sinking down in my chair, hoping I would not be called on, believing that if I could truly turn invisible, my stress would subside.

Red pens haunted my day as each project, assessment, or discussion led to an unsatisfactory score with a nicely written note in red ink stating my work was wrong. Cs and Ds were the bane of my existence, and to be honest, I was just exhausted feeling like I was working so hard with no result.

In middle school, one afternoon before a student-led parent–teacher conference, I remember my teachers giving each student a list of topics. They instructed us to go through the list and circle areas we felt we did well on. I managed to cross out each of the listed items:

Reading (I have a D in this class. Nope!)

Writing (Not a chance! I can't spell.)

Social Studies (Remembering dates? Yeah right. I'll be lucky to get a C-.)

Science (Ugh, so much reading and thinking.)

Math (I still struggle with adding . . . so, nope!)

The only item left I was able to circle was that I was "nice."

I remember thinking, Really? Is that all I have going for me? That I was kind? Talk about a complete failure.

I wonder whether the act of using the term yet, understanding the idea of "failing forward," or working at my own pace to prove mastery (so I could have actually understood how thoroughly understanding a topic felt) would have significantly changed my pathway throughout the education shuffle.

Traditional educational structures seem to shuffle students from one grade to the next regardless of their levels of understanding. Eventually, we end up with kids who have such large gaps in understanding, the simple act of showing up to class as a sophomore in high school seems too challenging, and students become disengaged and unmotivated.

"Why should I attend that class anyway? I barely understand what the teacher is talking about."

"Why should I do my homework? It will take me twice as long as it should, and I won't earn a passing grade anyway."

"Why should I take physics? I am no good at science or math. It will just be another *F* on my report card."

We need to break this cycle and help our students see failure as an opportunity to learn. We need to change our language in the classroom and begin focusing on the process students must follow for effective learning. Failure is a part of that process. The act of attempting a skill, failing, and having permission to reflect on the failure to try again is the way problem-solving, passionate innovators are built.

Isn't that exactly what we want to create in our students? Problem-solving skills? Passion for learning and discovery? Innovative minds?

Getting to that point with students isn't always easy. Sometimes you need to pull up immense reserves of patience and persistence.

Tiff: *Terrel was a challenge. There is no getting around that. Every day that he came into my class, he would toss his book bag (which students were not technically allowed to have with them) across the room, flop down in a chair, and immediately put his head on his desk.*

I worked with Terrel for three years and saw him become more and more withdrawn each year that passed. He was emotionally beat down every single day in his regular academic classes, and he had no coping skills. His behavior struggles often resulted in his removal from class, which would make him miss key content. When he returned to class, he was lost and confused, which inevitably caused another behavior burst, and the cycle continued again and again.

I never knew whom I was going to get when Terrel came to my room. Would it be calm Terrel, who could use his incredible mind to think and problem solve? Or would it be the Terrel who was so emotionally on edge that every moment of class was a battle?

Failure was the norm for Terrel. At the time, he had failing grades in almost every class, and it had gotten to the point that his teachers had honestly stopped trying. If he got through a class without throwing something across the room, it was a good day, in their minds.

Tiff: *That just wasn't good enough for me. I was not going to accept the fact that Terrel wouldn't learn, and I wasn't going to let him accept it either. In my classroom we use a student-paced mastery approach to instruction that lets students move at their own paces through content, proving their understanding each step of the way before they are allowed to move on.*

I will never forget the learning target students worked on that finally broke through to Terrel in my class: additive angles.

Oof!

Terrel came up against problems like this: "If <xyz is 30°, and <xym is 180°, how many degrees is <zym?" Let's just say it wasn't going well. He gave up after five minutes, and immediately his head went down to the table.

I tried gentle prompting. I offered one-on-one help. I told him I believed in him and knew he could figure it out. By the end of class, he had accomplished only those first five minutes of work. For the rest of class time, he was completely shut down.

The next day comes and Terrel is back in my room. Because students move at their own pace in my classroom, he is right back in that same task, working with additive angles again. This time, I get ten minutes of work out of him, and he actually watches me solve an example problem before he falls apart. The rest of the week looked like this:

Day 3: Terrel attempts the assessment for the skill and earns a 36 percent. He flops down on the classroom floor and refuses to speak to me for the rest of class. Right before students leave, he says, "Why do I have to keep doing this over and over again?"

My reply: "Because I know you can understand it."

Day 4: Terrel ignores me for twenty minutes and then finally watches me solve several example problems, even joining in the conversation a little bit sometimes. He takes the assessment again and earns a grade of 53 percent. He ends the class with flopping and eye rolls and even some growls.

Day 5: Terrel comes in, works through two examples with me, and says he is ready to take the assessment again.

The tool Terrel was using for the assessment let me track his progress as he went. He was sitting across my desk from me, his computer screen blocking most of his face. I watch my monitor as he submits his answer for the first question: It's correct! Second question: correct! Third, fourth, fifth: all correct!

At this moment, I start to get excited. This might be his success moment! I start to subtly watch his eyes as he is working (the only part of his face I can see). My computer tells me the exact moment that he submits the quiz and earns an 87 percent, surpassing the required score of 80 percent to move on to the next step of his individualized learning path.

Terrel is trying his very best to play it cool, to not show emotion, and hide the joy he feels at this success. But I can see it. The corners of his eyes crinkle, he looks down to try to hide his smile further behind the computer screen, and it is as if I can see the weight of his failure lift off his shoulders.

The boy stood taller that day as I calmly recognized his success with a huge smile on my face and gave him my signature to let him move on to the next step in learning.

––––––––

It would be a lie to tell you that this moment changed Terrel as a student. He still struggled. He still got in fights and was kicked out of his homeroom class more days than not. But from that moment on, when he came into Tiffany's classroom, his shoulders straightened. He no longer threw his book bag across the room and flopped down on the classroom floor in frustration (most of the time, at least).

It was a start. A beginning. A moment when failure became the stepping-stone to success for him instead of an insurmountable wall.

IS FAILURE EASIER THAN SUCCESS?

Failure should never mean the end of a lesson; instead, it should be the first step in growth. Failure simply tells us that some kind of feedback and corrective action is required, and additional effort is needed. All too often, the failure that happens in our classrooms acts not as a motivator but as a confirmation of the child's belief in their inability to succeed.

Consider the student that you have (we have all had one, several, or many) who is unmotivated. The one who refuses to work in your classroom and does everything in his or her power to avoid work. There is a good chance that this student has just done some simple math. They have come to an

FIRST ATTEMPT IN LEARNING

Want to reinforce a philosophy of failing positively in your classroom? Grab a free poster at teachbetter.com/BookResources.

important conclusion, a simple truth, from their time so far in school: It's a lot less work to fail than it is to succeed.

Consider this child in the early years of his or her education. Perhaps she took her first math test in first or second grade. She got a low score on it and felt the sting of failure. The class then moved on to the next unit. As the next assessment approaches, the student works hard, practices, and attacks the exam with confidence.

Unfortunately, it doesn't work out so well for her. There are still gaps in her understanding, and the next test comes back with a failing score again.

Maybe, when this student moves on to the next grade, she'll start the school year with positivity. This will be the year she succeeds! This will be the moment she shines. But again, the gaps in her understanding set her up for more struggle.

Students can work really hard and fail. They brush off their shoulders, practice all week, and fail. Every time they work hard, they fail. Again, and again, and again.

Eventually, the following is bound to happen: The student has an upcoming test and is simply exhausted. She is tired of studying and studying and failing. She is tired of working hard and still doing poorly, so she simply doesn't study. And what happens? She fails!

Think about the internal monologue that happens in this situation:

I tried really hard on the first three tests, and I failed. I didn't try at all on that last one, and I failed. So if I don't try, the result is the same as when I try really hard. Why do all that work?

If you consider students in middle or high school, it is no wonder they have lost the motivation to reach the potential we know they can achieve. Every time they've tried and failed, we gave them their *F* and moved on. We essentially said, *Nice try, but you're dumb.*

Now, I know we didn't actually say that to them, but that's how they feel it. "I tried really hard. I failed. I must be dumb." When that happens over and over again, year after year, a student is going to start to believe that voice in the back of his or her mind: *I must be dumb.*

This has to change. The story our students' experience that leads them to the conclusion that failure is easier than success has to be rewritten.

YOU FAILED! HOORAY!

Surely by now you have shifted your understanding of failure. We have laid out the reasons students choose to fail rather than try. You see the journey that transforms an eager first grader into a sullen and withdrawn eighth grader.

Now what? It's all well and good to understand the story, but understanding how to change the path your students are on is the goal of this chapter. We want to lay out some ideas for you to try. There is no guarantee that any single idea that follows will make that transformation happen in a single day, week, or year. Shifting this mindset in students takes time and effort. But the sooner you start working toward the shift, the sooner you will start to see results.

You should be aware that you will see varying levels of success depending on the ages of your students. If you are working with very young students (early elementary), these shifts will happen more quickly because they are far more adaptable and have fewer negative failure experiences when they are younger.

Once you hit upper elementary and middle school, some of these failure patterns start to become firmly ingrained in their brains, and it becomes a more difficult, painful process to change them.

In high school students, your mission can seem impossible. You may not see the results of your hard work in a year or even throughout the child's high school career. It is so vitally important, however, that you keep up the stamina, hard work, and enthusiasm for failure.

Often, teenagers with a failure mindset have been failing ineffectively for nearly a decade. That is a hard pattern to reset! This makes it all the more crucial for you to be consistent, passionate, and stubborn in your celebration of failure as a launching point. If you believe in them and their power to succeed through failure, they will remember it ten years down the road. It will shape their lives positively even if you can't see it.

How do we do it? How do we transform the way our students view failure?

Some of the suggestions below are easy. Some are quite involved and will require you to shift most of what you do in your class. Start with just one. Once you feel like you have that down, move on to the next. Revisit this chapter every few months and ask yourself what more you can do from this list of ideas.

Just as success for our students doesn't happen overnight, success for us takes time. As long as you are continuously pushing yourself to be better today than you were yesterday and better tomorrow than you are today, you are on the right track.

1. Celebrate failure

Tiffany loves failure. If you ever visit her classroom, you will see evidence of this almost immediately. It doesn't involve any fancy curriculum or massive shifts in how and what she teaches. She celebrates failure in a very simple, easy-to-emulate way. Try this the next time a student fails in your class:

_____

Tiff: *"WOO HOO! YOU FAILED!"*

This phrase comes charging out of my mouth at least once a day, and I shout it at a level that probably annoys my teaching neighbors. It is often accompanied by some jumping up and down, high fiving, and clapping. It is not a quiet celebration or a pat on the back. It is a fiery, loud, startling, and intense moment of celebration, sometimes accompanied by a dance party.

The first time each year that I celebrate in this way, I inevitably see a room full of stares, confusion, and tilted heads (kind of like when you ask your dog if he wants to go for a walk and he looks at you quizzically).

Eventually, a student in the room giggles a little bit and says, "What?"

Ah! My opening! I then launch into an enthusiastic (and yes, still loud) explanation of how excited I am that they have failed. I tell them it is completely awesome that they failed because now I get to actually do my job: I get to help them learn.

_____

When you can show your students that you are excited to help them learn, even (and especially) when they have failed initially, the feeling becomes contagious. Flipping the script you use when talking with students is the first and, we would argue, most important step you can take.

Within a few weeks of consistently reacting this way, you will start to notice a transformation in your students and your classroom. You will know you have achieved the first step in building a healthy response to failure when you start to hear students celebrating failure themselves. There is something wonderful about overhearing a student congratulating another student on failing and then seeing them work together, knowing they will have multiple attempts to show they understand.

Which leads us to the second point.

2. Multiple attempts to show understanding

It is time to think about retakes. This is a hot topic among educators, and both sides of the issue will argue fiercely about the pros and cons of retakes.

Does allowing retakes encourage laziness?

What if every single student wants a retake?

The real world doesn't offer retakes!

The real world does offer retakes!

When do you say enough is enough?

What if they retake it over and over again and never get better?

Isn't this a lot of extra work for me?

I don't want to enable my students to be lazy!

Each one of these items could justify a full chapter if not a full book! Suffice it to say, there are many opinions on the topic and many strong feelings. The four of us firmly believe that reassessment should be not only allowed but required if a student has not yet met the desired level of mastery. If we accept a student's initial low score, we accept failure as the end. If we make reassessment a fundamental principle in our classrooms, we build a culture of pushing forward, perseverance, and hope.

We freely acknowledge that retakes can be a source of unneeded stress if not implemented properly. You absolutely need to create a system for how they work in your classroom. A few things to consider might be . . .

- Could requiring students to request a retake make the process more manageable?
- When can a student request a retake?
- What must a student do to be given a retake?
- What happens between the first failure and the retake?
- What happens after the retake if the student still does not show mastery?

Retakes offer incredible possibilities for better teaching and better learning. Try not to dismiss them offhand, but thoughtfully consider how you can actually make them work for you and your students.

3. Reflection and relearning

A student failing in your classroom, celebrating that failure, and being given another attempt to learn is not the end of the plan. There must be reflection and redirection. When a student makes a mistake, she should reflect on what went wrong, where she got confused, and how to correct it moving forward. This reflection is what makes failure so important. Like Tiffany says, this is where we get to do our jobs. This is where we get to teach them and where they get to learn!

We have often seen teachers require students to complete test or quiz corrections, and we agree that this can be an important piece of the puzzle, but we would like to offer a word of caution: **Do not allow the focus of reflection to be on task completion.**

It is actually quite easy for a student to look up answers that they missed and put those down on their corrections. It is generally a task that requires minimal thought, and the information recorded on the correction is right back out of the brain in minutes. If we shift the purpose and focus of corrections on actual learning, we can see more success. Here are some quick thoughts on how you might do this:

- Require a reflection for each missed question that asks students to explain what they misunderstood and where they went wrong in the questions.
- Use the reflection to guide the next steps for the student.

  - Trouble remembering vocabulary words? Instruct students to make flashcards and help them learn how to study effectively.
  - Misunderstood a concept? Encourage them to seek out other explanations or resources to help them understand. YouTube can be a good option for this, as can their peers.
  - Careless errors? Ask them to go back and identify exactly what each careless error was and where in the question they made the error. (This works very well for math!) Have them keep a log of the kinds of careless errors they make. When they have to add "silly addition error" to the log for the fifteenth time in a week, they are more likely to prevent that error next time!

- Conference with the student, spot checking their new understanding before moving on. Again, completing the corrections is NOT the goal. Learning from them is.

4. Revolutionary change

There comes a point when steps one through three have done all they can do in your classroom, and you find that it is time to push even further. Some teachers choose to dive right in with steps one through four all at once. If that suits you, go for it! If not, a gradual approach is also fine.

Whenever you are ready, though, the big leap you take now is to look at every single aspect of your teaching and ask yourself, *Is this helping students grow in a positive way through failure?*

- Can you adjust the pacing of your class so every student moves through the content at their own pace?

- Are you willing to stubbornly refuse to allow a student to move on until they understand the content?
- Are you willing to remove yourself from the role of content deliverer so you can devote class time to work with individuals and small groups?
- Can you start from scratch, objectively examining everything you do as a teacher and what pieces of it need to stay or go?
- Will you reach out to others in the field who have made these changes and can help you reimagine today's classrooms?

START SOMEWHERE

It doesn't matter much to us which step you begin with or how quickly you move through them. We don't care if you do them in order or bob back and forth between steps. The only thing that matters is that you start somewhere. We are just as fearful of failure as our students are. As teachers, we aren't generally big fans of switching up what we do, and the reason why comes down to one very simple idea: We fear failure ourselves.

It is time to embrace that you will fail in your efforts to help students learn and grow from failure. It is time to accept that it will happen. Once we are willing to risk failure, we are finally ready to grow.

STORIES FROM THE TEACH BETTER COMMUNITY

> YES, IT'S A STORY ABOUT PALM PILOTS: THOMAS C. MURRAY (@THOMASCMURRAY)
Director of innovation, Future Ready Schools®

In the spring of 2002, I was teaching fourth grade and in my second year of teaching. It's hard to believe, but in 2002, my classroom was 1:1. No, not laptops—Palm Pilots. Remember those things? A few weeks into the pilot project, I had a planned, formal observation. Like any teacher, I wanted to impress my principal.

The date came, and my observation lesson was ready to go. It was a thirty-minute spelling lesson. (Don't judge—but, yes, really!) After reviewing the Palm Pilot expectations and the software we'd be using, we dove in. For most of the lesson, students practiced their individualized spelling lists with partners. One partner would read another's spelling word. They would then write their spelling word using the new Graffity program on the Palm Pilot and beam it back to their partner to verify their answer. For the entire lesson, students were engaged, my lesson plan was followed perfectly, and technology was used the entire time. In my mind, I had crushed it!

The following day, all fired up, I walked down to my principal's office for the post observation. I was excited to hear how great he thought my lesson had been the day before. I sat down, and as he always would, my principal made me feel welcome. Again, he created a culture where people wanted to be. A culture where people could take risks. He looked at me and started like every principal has: "So Tom, how do YOU think the lesson went?"

I remember being excited to share. "Well, I think it went really well. Kids were 100 percent engaged. Technology was used the entire time. My lesson plan was followed almost to the minute. Kids were on task. Honestly, I think it went really well."

He smiled, looked at me, and said, "So Tom, what were your learning objectives?"

"We wanted to use the Palm Pilots to be able to . . ." I began.

He cut me off. "No, Tom, what were your learning objectives?"

Hmmm. Maybe he misunderstood. "We wanted to use the Palm Pilots to . . ."

He cut me off again. "Tom, let me push you on this. Every time I ask you about learning, you start talking about technology." Although he also shared a variety of positives, he also stated, "I honestly think you created that lesson because the technology could do something, not because it was the best way to learn something."

Wow.

I can honestly say that it was that instructional supervision conversation that fundamentally changed how I viewed the role of technology in the classroom. My mindset was to celebrate the technology use. I could have done the exact same things, with paper and pencil, in far less time, and experienced the exact same learning outcomes. I remained hyper-focused on the tools, and ultimately lost sight of what was most important—the learning.

This was only one of the many times I failed forward as a classroom teacher, but I appreciate the mentors and those that helped me get better along the way!

CHAPTER 6
EXPECT BETTER

"SET YOUR CLASSROOM EXPECTATIONS HIGH, THE HIGHER THE BETTER. EXPECT THE MOST FANTASTIC THINGS TO HAPPEN, NOT IN THE FUTURE BUT RIGHT NOW!"

–ROBERT JOHN MEEHAN, TEACHER'S JOURNEY

What we believe about other human beings has the power to change their beliefs in themselves, their beliefs in us, and the course of their futures. We are sure we aren't the first ones to tell you that your impact on young people is something that simply cannot be understated. And we don't doubt that you understand this impact and want to make sure it is a positive one. Why else would you be reading this book?

Sometimes, though, our hopes for what we can accomplish with our students and the visions we have for the kinds of teachers we can be can get a little bit cloudy. We must never lose sight of the immense power we possess, power that has the potential for either inspiring outcomes or disheartening results.

Although Jeff does not come from an education background in a traditional sense, he has been working with young people and educators for most of his life. At one point, he coached high school soccer for four years. During his second season coaching, he had an autistic player, Jason, on his team. This circumstance was new to Jeff, as he'd had no experience with an autistic person. He did not know much about it or the struggles that come with it. He remembers how, at the start of preseason practices, this player's mom offered him some tips for working with her son.

———————

Jeff: The first several practices went smoothly, and I pretty much forgot about that conversation. Jason had been doing well. You see, in the first few weeks of practice, we weren't allowed to use balls; they had to just be focused on conditioning.

As soon as we incorporated foot skills into practices, Jason started to struggle. As he struggled, he started to get upset—almost angry—at the ball, at his teammates, at me, and above all, at himself.

I forgot everything his mom had told me. To be honest, I forgot he was even autistic.

All I saw was a fifteen-year-old kid who was frustrated.

One day at practice, Jason was struggling more than usual with a particular drill that consisted of quite a bit of dribbling. If you're not familiar with dribbling in soccer, it is when you move with the ball using quick, light touches on the ball to keep it close to you and avoid losing it. It's a skill that takes a lot of work and is a common area of struggle for younger players. Jason wasn't the only one having trouble keeping control of the ball, but his frustration was showing more than anyone else.

I started to worry he might give up.

———————

We have all seen this student in our classes, and we would be shocked if you told us that you never had. Whether it is a third grader struggling with math facts or a high school student who can't quite grasp essay writing, seeing our students struggle is not new to us. We may know that the student is capable and that they just need the right combination of advice, support, and motivation, but it isn't always easy to bring the stars in alignment to give this child what he or she needs.

We suspect that there isn't a teacher in the world who hasn't at some point felt like one of their students might just never get it. Nothing is working. Nothing has worked. Believing that something—anything—could work seems impossible.

We've all been there. It's okay to get frustrated, to get stressed. It's human nature, and this isn't an easy situation. Don't give up. Don't let go of your belief in the student. There is a key that will unlock the puzzle. There is a way.

Jeff: *Seeing Jason's frustration increase one day, I stopped practice and brought my most skilled player in front of the team with me. I had him show everyone how to do the drill. I then brought Jason up with us, and I had him try. He got tripped up, lost control of the ball, and hung his head in shame, furious with himself.*

Now, I had built a very strong relationship with all of my players. I was huge on teamwork and unity. We had a rule on our team: we do everything as a team—everything. There were no individuals, just a team.

I would lead the team in calls back and forth:

"If Tim scores a goal, who scores?"

"The team!"

"If Joe gets scored on, whose fault is it?"

"The team!"

"When we win . . . "

"We win as a team!"

"When we lose . . . "

"We lose as a team!"

So I asked them, "If Jason loses the ball, who loses the ball?"

They replied as usual, "The team!"

I asked another, "Who will help Jason be better at control?"

"The team!"

Finally, I asked, "Who here believes Jason can do this drill?"

"The team!"

Jason's face lit up. He looked at me with a determination usually reserved for the movies. I sent the team back to the starting lines, and we began to run the drill again. I was so pumped up. The look on his face told me he was about to rock out this drill. He felt supported; he knew we believed he could do it.

Jason lost control again. And again. And again. And again . . . .

———

There is no magical solution. Your strategies and efforts are often not going to work the first time or the fifth or even the fiftieth! There are times when we need to go back to the drawing board or patiently and stubbornly wade through the process that it takes for a student to get where you know they can get. And sometimes the goal of our stubborn belief in our students' abilities to rise to our expectations can have outcomes far beyond what we expected.

Jeff: Jason got frustrated, even angry, from time to time. He actually struggled with that drill pretty much all season. I could have easily chalked it up as a loss for me as a coach, but Jason did something that changed the way I viewed things forever: He never gave up. He never lost that look of determination. He just kept trying and trying and trying.

Jason never became a great ball handler, and he was never one of my best players. He also never gave up. He always pushed as hard as he could, and he became a strong member of our team. He was a source of strength for us because he would never let anyone else give up either. After hearing his teammates telling him again and again, "You've got this! Don't give up!" He would repeat the same to them any time they looked tired or frustrated or lost the ball.

And he hustled! Oh man, did he hustle.

He annoyed the heck out of the other teams during games. I'd put him in, and he would just buzz all around them, never stopping. It drove our opponents nuts!

I never thought of Jason as "my player with autism." He was just another one of my players and one who fought hard for me every single day.

At the end of that season, Jason's mom thanked me for being so great with him, and I sort of shrugged it off. I told her he was a good kid who worked really hard.

It wasn't until many years after that day in practice, long after the season had ended, that Jeff realized what he had witnessed. He saw a frustrated child, who had more day-to-day struggles than most, fight through that frustration and never give up because his team and his coach believed in him.

Long after Jason had moved past the soccer team and ahead to the rest of his life, Jeff remembered the advice Jason's mom gave him at the start of the season: "He just needs to know you believe he can do it."

"MY STUDENTS CAN'T DO THIS . . . "

The four of us work with educators from all around the country, even around the world. We see a lot of things—good, bad, and everything in between. We have had hundreds of thousands of conversations with educators in just about every situation you can imagine. The phrase "my students can't do this" ranks high up on the list of "Things We Hate to Hear Come out of Teachers' Mouths."

Unfortunately, it is also something we hear pretty often. When you spend time in schools, whether it is as an employee, an administrator, or a trainer, you are bound to get some pushback on the new idea you want people to try.

Have you said those words out loud? In a meeting? In a private conversation? In your own mind? Don't worry. It's okay. Human beings have an amazing ability to be flexible—to change, adapt, and grow. And we are here to give you that extra push you need to take that leap.

You see, we know that the students sitting in our classrooms, in your classroom, and in classrooms all over the world are capable of incredible, amazing, inspiring things. We know that it is hard to see this potential in some of the students we work with. We have been there!

The kind of unbreakable belief in our students and commitment to expecting their success is not something that comes easily or naturally. It requires work, reflection, and commitment. It is not something that we all succeed at every minute of every day in our careers.

Believe us, you are not alone.

Even the four of us writing this book have been guilty of that kind of thinking. We have all had moments when all we wanted, all we expected, was that our students would simply write their names on their papers and not cause chaos in our classes. We have had moments when we expected less of our students because fighting for those expectations is hard. Changing that thinking and changing our approaches are hard to do. Impossibly hard!

Rae: *The first time I came across The Grid Method, I remember actually thinking to myself,* This is a great idea, but I don't have the time to target my lessons toward students like this. And let's be realistic; they probably can't handle a self-paced model anyway. They are only sixth graders.

At the time, I had one of the more challenging groups of my career. To be honest, it was a successful day if I could just get through a short mini lesson. I hate to admit it, but managing behavior was my focus, and academics came second—a distant second. Entertaining the idea that this group would be capable of taking ownership over their learning was ridiculous. Not to mention having to somehow explain this drastic change to parents . . .

It seemed like too big of a bite to chew.

I struggled with this for a while, going back and forth between deciding to try this new model of student-paced learning or stick to the damage control I had been striving for so far that year.

———

Once you're past the "new teacher scramble" of those first few years of your career, you can fall into a common trap. When we get into a groove or routine, we can unintentionally reach a plateau, where we can start to settle for just getting by, just doing our jobs.

This happens to us all because once we have that opportunity to actually come up for air, it's natural to relax in the comfort of what you know how to do. At this point we can make one of the most important decisions of our careers: Are we satisfied with being good enough, or do we want to be great? Do we want to be transformative? Have we reached the end of our growth as educators, or are we going to push through and be better today than we were yesterday?

———

Rae: *I was a few years into my career, and I considered myself a pretty good educator. I was building relationships with my students, getting involved in leadership roles in my school building, and had begun welcoming student teachers into my classroom on a regular basis.*

I was also excited about continuing my work with Teach Further, an approach I developed for unit planning that was helping educators around the country connect content with community stakeholders through themed internships. And because of my work in this area, I was getting opportunities to work with and train teachers on how to duplicate this innovation in their classrooms.

With all this going on, I had to decide whether I was finished taking on challenges that I knew were best for students.

It was time to change my mindset and banish the statement "My students can't do this" from my mind.

———

We all see our students struggle. We all see behavior problems and deficient reading skills. We all see failure to think independently and communicate. It is easy and natural for us to start to believe that our students can't handle innovative learning experiences, because they haven't shown us they can.

We've all thought this at some point whether with a particular student or several students. We might come up with a new idea ourselves, or perhaps a new initiative is presented to us, and we immediately start picturing that one student or group of students we think will struggle with it. (You can probably picture one of them right now!) Maybe we incorporate a new system or routine in our classroom, and that one student seems to be the only one who can't figure it out. We sometimes start to think *Well, yeah. I didn't really think he could do it in the first place.*

Although it is fairly common, not to mention understandable, to consider those students and their potential struggles, we must avoid assuming that because they struggle with something, they will not be successful in the future or in other areas.

If a student struggles with sitting still in class, that doesn't mean he can't benefit from an engaging, interactive lesson on fractions.

If a student doesn't ever turn in homework, it doesn't mean she can't thrive in a self-paced learning environment.

If a student has never been "good at school," it doesn't mean he can't be.

When we believe that these students can't do it, that they can't benefit from some new instructional method because they can't handle it, we set them up for failure before we even start.

Chad spends a huge amount of time traveling from school to school, working with educators and coaching administration to help bring student-paced mastery learning to classrooms all over the place. He hears "My students can't do this" on a regular basis. Consider the reply he often gives when challenging this kind of thinking:

"If they can't do it, maybe it's because a teacher before you thought the same thing. And the teacher before that teacher thought the same thing too. Perhaps those students can't do it because they have never truly been given a chance to do it. Perhaps you are becoming another in a long line of teachers who do not believe in what their students can do."

This idea is near and dear to Chad's heart; in fact, a student he worked with years ago made a lasting impact that shaped Chad's purpose and focus significantly.

––––––

Chad: You know, we all have this kid sitting in our classroom. I knew Jesse was that kid. I knew a few things about Jesse: He had been diagnosed with oppositional defiant disorder, he was reading at a third-grade level as an eighth grader, and he struggled with controlling his emotions.

Because he couldn't read very well, he'd get frustrated. Since he couldn't control his emotions when he got angry, he would do dumb stuff and get kicked out of class. I had Jesse in the last period of the day, so there were many days when I did not get to see him at all.

At one point, it had been almost two weeks since I'd had Jesse in my classroom, so I asked my colleagues if he had left our district. Turns out, Jesse had just been getting kicked out of earlier classes every single day. This wasn't okay with me. I mean, I knew he was a challenge, but I wasn't even getting the opportunity to try to reach him. So I asked my colleagues and my admin if I could get Jesse every day.

Their first question was simply "why?" I explained that I was trying something new, and I wanted to have the chance to at least try to help Jesse. So we made a deal that I could get him from in-school suspension, but he needed to stay in my room unless there were severe issues.

I knew that if I could let him struggle and provide him with the support that he needed, he could succeed. Every day I would walk up to in-school suspension and would look at Jesse and say, "Jesse, are you going to work for me today?"

Jesse would look at me and say, "Yeah, Coach O, I'll work for you."

So Jesse started going to Chad's class, working through his Grids, and started showing improvement; in fact, he started to succeed, to thrive! Jesse was now succeeding in Chad's class even when he was struggling to not get kicked out of other classes. He even got to take on a leadership role from time to time as a classroom "genius" and help other students out. This was a huge deal for him; no one had ever asked Jesse to be a leader.

Chad: *Jesse was one of those kids whom people just wrote off. He's the kid that the teachers from the grade before warn you about before the school year starts.*

But the approach I took in my classroom allowed Jesse to struggle without that struggle being the end of his journey. Because I used a mastery learning approach, and everyone worked at their individual paces, I could read out loud to him when he needed it. I could give him extra help. I could give him multiple chances to succeed.

He started taking those opportunities. He started working longer because he was feeling success.

Jesse was no longer unreachable.

At the end of the year, I got called down to the office. The secretary said, "Mr. Ostrowski, Jesse's mother is here." My first thought was Oh no! What did I do? *(We've all been there, right?)*

I walked down to the office, and this woman gave me the biggest hug I have ever gotten in my life from someone who isn't my wife.

"Mr. Ostrowski, Jesse got a B."

"Yea, I know. He's been doing really well."

"But he got a B! He's never gotten a B in any class."

"Well, he's been working really hard. Doing really well."

Then she pulled me away and got very serious with me. "You don't understand. My son does not get Bs. He doesn't do good in school."

I looked her in the eyes and simply said, "He does now."

You see, one of the most powerful things we can do for our students is to simply believe in them. Even when they have given us hundreds of reasons to assume they cannot do that new thing, we need to believe they can. Those students you are thinking of right now, about whom you've maybe thought this way before? Most likely you are not the first to think that way, feel like that, or doubt them. There's a good chance at least one of their earlier teachers had also assumed they couldn't do something. We have to end this cycle in which "those kids" continue to be looked at as "those kids" and expected to fail; instead, we need to flip the script and believe in them!

So we challenge you: Find your Jesse. Find a way to believe in his or her ability to grow, power to learn, and power to excel.

We need to stress again, if these stories of belief make you feel subpar, if you recognize a little bit too much truth in the stories of teachers who have lowered their expectations for students, it does not make you a bad teacher, and it doesn't mean the ones who came before in the long line of teachers in a child's life were bad teachers either.

Remember, the Teach Better mindset is not about going from being a bad teacher to a great teacher. It is about continuously striving to be better than you were yesterday. When you pause and reflect on things you've done in the past, things that you could have done better, don't beat yourself up. Take that opportunity, learn from it, grow, and be better next time.

This is easier said than done, we know, but dig deep and remember that there are always reasons for every struggle a student has. Our job is to figure out what those reasons are and provide support and guidance for overcoming those obstacles. Your belief in them can be the fuel that will power those students' abilities to succeed!

MAKE THE SHIFT. EXPECT MORE.

The next time a new initiative comes along, and you start to picture that student who is going to struggle with it, flip your thinking. Recognize your low expectations, make a game plan to counteract those thoughts, and help those students succeed. Map out the path of their potential struggles (you probably already know where they will have difficulty), and create a plan for how to guide them along the way. Most importantly, believe that they can do it, and never, ever stop telling them that you believe in them.

When students believe they can do something, they will try harder, and small setbacks will be less likely to negatively affect their efforts, or at least they will have a smaller impact on those efforts. And when students believe that you believe they can do something, they are much more likely to believe it themselves. More importantly, when you believe they can do it, you will not stop until you help them succeed. And that is powerful.

Tiff: Oh, Terrel . . . the headaches and joy you gave me during our three years together!

Terrel had a long history of disruptive behavior, suspension, fighting, talking back to teachers, and significant underachievement. He had, in fact, qualified for gifted services that indicated his intellectual ability was quite high, something that went unacknowledged by many of the adults who worked with him but also placed him in my classroom for forty-five minutes each day.

On informing his teachers of this placement, one of them looked at me with a sneer on her face and said, "There is no way that kid is actually gifted. He must have cheated on that test."

Whoa! Talk about having low expectations for your students!

STRENGTHENING YOUR BELIEF MUSCLES

It is simply not enough to read this book and tell yourself you will believe in your students. You need to work at it. You need to invest in it. Make it a primary focus every single day.

Negativity swirls all around us while we're in the halls of our buildings. There is no escaping the fact that some of your colleagues will try to (sometimes unknowingly) tear down your positivity and your beliefs. They will assure you that David is simply not smart enough to grasp geometry, or that Emma is not the type of student who will ever follow that new procedure. This does not make them bad people or bad teachers. It simply makes them a challenge you will need to overcome. We encourage you to help them see the errors of their ways, but more importantly, you must not let that negativity change your belief.

––––––––

Tiff: *"John is hopeless."*

"Michael cries over everything."

"Angie won't focus on anything."

"Shenae is always looking for trouble."

"Brady just isn't a good reader."

I have sat in hundreds of meetings as a teacher. Faculty meetings, grade-level meetings, department meetings. Meetings galore! It constantly shocks me how often sentences like these come out of the mouths of educators.

I understand that some of these comments are often born of exhaustion and frustration. They may come from a teacher not feeling well or dealing with a personal struggle. But every one of them is still a judgment and criticism of a student. Each of them is a resignation to a student's inability to accomplish something whether it's math, behavior management, or attention. Many of them come from a place where teachers have lost the commitment to expect better of their students.

One meeting stands out in particular. I was working with elementary teachers, and we were analyzing data and progress for students studying paragraph writing. The meeting was scheduled for fifty minutes. The first ten minutes were primarily made up of chitchat and catching up. Then we looked at data from a pre-assessment for the next ten minutes. This is where things started to turn ugly.

Criticisms of the students, their previous teachers, their parents, the administration, and pretty much every other human being involved with the education of children began flying around the room.

Multiple voices blamed everything they could think of for why these students couldn't learn. Yes! They actual said "couldn't"!

I interjected with a simple comment: "I don't think any of that is true. I believe these students can learn. If we don't believe it, how will they?"

If I were a magical sorceress with powers to change mindsets with just some simple words, they all would have had a change of heart and made an about-face in their thinking about these kids. But I am not, and they did not.

Instead, I was met with silent stares, no eye contact, sighs, and eye rolls, and the conversation continued.

Let's just say I had my work cut out for me. It was time to build positive relationships with teachers. I needed to see them where they were and help them find hope in the struggle. It wasn't time to give up on them, to lose my belief in these amazing educators. It was time for me to believe in their own power to grow and change.

It was time to expect better of my colleagues.

––––––––––

There is a myth that says you can only stay positive for so long in a negative environment, that eventually it will beat you down and make you jaded. You might think your school is filled with so much negativity that you will only be able to hold on to your positivity and beliefs for so long.

This simply is not the case. You absolutely can hold on to that belief. You can overcome the negativity. It will not be easy, but the truth is, the more you have to fight to overcome negativity, the stronger your belief will become. Every time you push past a colleague's feeling that "these kids will never get this," your own belief grows. Every time you look at the student that no one else thinks can succeed and see the potential in them, your belief will strengthen. This doesn't mean you won't have bad days when you doubt your students or yourself or when you let others' lack of faith creep into your head. And it doesn't mean you will always believe in every student the way you should.

Belief and positivity are a lot like the muscles in your body. You can work hard on them, exercising every day, but that doesn't mean they will never ache. It doesn't mean they will always be strong enough to lift every obstacle. And it doesn't mean it will always feel like they're actually getting stronger. But if you stay focused on your workouts and push through the soreness, aches, and pains, those muscles will get stronger, and those same workouts you struggled with will become easier to master.

Just like those muscles, you must continually focus on your positivity and the belief in your students. It will not always be easy. You will face struggles, and you will doubt your ability to keep it up. Stay focused. Stay consistent. When you push through the soreness (the negativity) and those aches and pains (the small failures along the way and the colleagues who fight your positivity), you will grow. You will become stronger. And you will find it easier and easier to block out the naysayers and see the potential in every student who enters your classroom.

Expecting better goes beyond simply believing that our students can achieve success. We must also believe we can succeed. You see, when we say, "this kid will just never get this," what we're really saying is, "I'm not good enough to help her get this." And that is simply not true.

You can lead your students, even those who struggle the most, to success. You can guide them as they find their way. You can help them as they struggle and grow.

You will help them succeed.

You will also struggle with this just as much as your students struggle with new content. You will get tripped up, fall on your face, and feel bruised, but you will get back up, you will reflect, you will adjust, and you will find a new way to reach those hard-to-reach students. You will do this because you are an amazing educator who is so passionate about what you do, nothing can stop you!

BEYOND YOUR STUDENTS: YOU AND YOUR JOURNEY

You may be comfortable with where you are in your career and your life. Maybe you have your routines in place. Maybe your students are scoring okay on standardized tests.

Student behavior is pretty good.

Parents don't complain too much.

Colleagues ask for your advice.

Administration pretty much leaves you alone.

Things are pretty okay.

To expect better, however, is to expect more for yourself. More of yourself. To expect that you can and will achieve more. Set high standards, chase big dreams, and believe that you will meet them!

The power of believing in your students is not a big secret. We're not going to sit here and claim we're the first to tell you to believe in them. Do a quick Google search, and you're bound to see twenty-five different stories of awesome teachers instilling belief in children and then watching the positive impacts.

This is not a bad thing. We just rambled on for several pages about believing in your students. It's crucial! They need to know they can achieve greatness so they will follow their dreams.

We sometimes forget, though, that we're all living our lives as well, chasing our own dreams, dealing with our own struggles, and facing our own challenges. As teachers, we can get so focused on our students—supporting their growth, going to the ends of the Earth to be there for them and do whatever it takes to pick them up and help them succeed—that we forget to spend any time on ourselves.

We're here to tell you, loud and clear: It is okay to focus on your personal growth.

Don't stop putting your energy and passion into your students. That's not what we're saying. But when you forget to do the same for yourself, you're actually providing less than your best to your students. Growing yourself, building on your strengths, and chasing your own dreams will positively impact those you serve.

If you have a dream of being an amazing teacher, focus on that. Take every opportunity you can to learn and grow. Be innovative. Be real. Never settle for "okay." Always be better today than you were yesterday.

If you have a goal of being an administrator, don't lose sight of that. Do not think because you want to be a principal and would need to leave the classroom that you care any less for your students; instead, realize how many more kids you can positively impact if you are able to help an entire building of teachers be better.

If you have the vision to create something to share with other educators and help them reach more students, don't let anyone tell you that makes you less of a teacher. Focus on the impact you can make and go get it!

"I'M JUST A TEACHER."

Ever said those words? It's okay; we all have. But we want you to shift your mindset and never think that way again. You see, it's easy for us to put ourselves in a box of just being a teacher. We don't usually look at this as a negative, and it's really not. Teaching is what we do. We're proud of what we do, and what we do is important. It's the "just" that we want you to get rid of.

You are not just a teacher. You are so much more.

Tiff: *I had an interesting experience a while back returning home from a confer-*
ence. I had to practically run out the door of the conference right after my presen-
tation, as I had a flight to catch and the turnaround time was, shall we say, a little
bit tight. Jeff was also at the conference presenting, and he drove me to the airport.

On the way, I received a text from the airline saying that the flight had been
delayed. On the one hand, this was a good thing, because it meant we did not have
to put our lives on the line racing down the highway. On the other hand, I had a
connecting flight to catch, which also happened to have a very short turnaround
time, so I was not going to make that connection.

When we got to the airport, my first stop was the airline desk. Before I could say, "I
think I might miss my connecting flight," the airline agent said, "We have a bus that's
going to be driving you to your destination in time to make your connection."

Taken aback, I barely blinked before she handed me my ticket and directed me
outside and down the road to catch my bus. I was relieved to be able to make my
connecting flight, as I had a workshop to run the next day, but I wasn't too thrilled
about a two-hour bus ride.

About thirty of us boarded the bus and made our way toward the next airport. We
all start chatting, typical small talk: "What do you do?" and "Where are you head-
ed?" All the usual conversations that happen when you're in a strange situation
with a bunch of strangers.

My turn came around, and a very friendly gentleman sitting across the aisle from
me asked, "So, what do you do?"

Perhaps some background information is appropriate at this point. At the
time, Tiffany had just made the decision to change positions for the upcoming
school year. She was an elementary school teacher working with gifted students
in third through fifth grade in math and reading, and less than a week before
this fateful bus ride, she had decided to accept a part-time position teaching
math to struggling ninth graders. The other half of her work week would be
dedicated to working with us at Teach Better.

This was a very new position for her, and she wasn't quite sure yet how to
describe it.

Tiff: After a brief whirlwind of thoughts, I replied, "I am an education consultant."

The gentleman paused and simply said, "Oh. Okay."

That was certainly not the reaction I have toward my career! I was tickled pink, over-the-moon excited about this amazing opportunity to change the world. But, let's admit it, my job description did not make it sound all that exciting.

In a frenzy, I immediately blurted out everything about my job that makes it the best job in the world. I wanted him to feel how amazing I felt about the whole situation.

"Wait! Actually what I do is travel the country, working with amazing educators on a mission to transform the world of teaching and learning and support the next generation of awesome leaders. I write, I speak, I share. I love it."

The man chuckled a bit, and said, "Well, that certainly does sound more interesting."

Education consultant sounds dry and boring. World changer and revolutionary? Much better.

WHAT DO YOU DO?

What's the point of Tiff's story? The fact is, we have heard the phrase "I'm just a teacher" come out of the mouths of many educators we've worked with.

So let's get something straight right now: You are not just a teacher. You are a life changer. You are a world changer. You are a leader, a role model, and one of the most important pieces of every one of your students' lives.

You make a difference.

Our words and our thoughts have power and can change not only the way the world sees us but the way we see ourselves. You see, the mission of education is truly to transform the world. Our goal every single day is to connect with students in ways that make them imagine the possibilities of life. We design experiences that help our students see the world for the amazing, complicated, troubled place that it is. We help our students design what our future will look like. We are not just teachers any more than Tiffany is just an education consultant. We are so much more than that. You are so much more than that.

We want you to change the way you answer the question, "What do you do?" Change the way you view yourself. Be bold in who you are and what you do.

What will you say the next time someone asks, "What do you do?"

"I am a teacher. I'm changing the world!"

BELIEVING THIS IS EASIER SAID THAN DONE

With all of the negativity that surrounds us, it can be difficult to have confidence in ourselves that we can achieve more. Maybe you've felt this way. Maybe someone has told you that you're "just a teacher." And while you wear that title proudly, you know you can do more, and you want to do more.

So how do we fight the thoughts that we aren't worthy or talented enough to chase those bigger dreams for ourselves?

————

Jeff: *I struggle with self-confidence. Most people have a hard time believing this because I put on a pretty good show most days, but there are a lot of days where I wake up wondering if I have what it takes, if I'm worthy of the success I want for myself, or whether I will ever actually achieve that success.*

To combat this internal struggle, I do two very important things. First, I try very hard to surround myself with positive people who care about me and stay away from people who are filled with negativity about life (easier said than done, I know).

Second, I journal every day. I use a simple app on my phone for this, but any type of journal will work. I add to my journal twice a day, once in the morning and once just before bed.

In the morning, I list "three things I am grateful for today." And then I write out my daily affirmations. These affirmations are crucial. At first, they will feel a bit silly, but I urge you to take them seriously and do them every day; furthermore, I strongly suggest you say them aloud as you write them.

To help you visualize, here are my affirmations (and yes, I say them aloud):

I am an awesome father.

I am an awesome husband.

I am an awesome leader.

I help teachers reach more students.

I am changing the world.

I will be successful.

I will give my family the life they deserve.

I will give myself the life I deserve.

Just before bedtime, I add "three amazing things that happened today." Yes, "amazing." Why? Because it can be difficult a lot of days to find three "amazing" things that happened, so it forces me to reflect on and appreciate what I've accomplished each day. These can be things like getting a certain task done, helping that one student get past a struggle, or spending some extra time with your family.

Finally, I list "three things that could have gone better today." This is the time for reflection on what you could have done better today, and it sets you up for tomorrow's goals. This could be something like "Johnny mastering the next learning objective in his personal learning path" or "Remembering to do XYZ."

This process has been a game changer for me. It took a while for it to become a solid part of my routine, but now that it is, it creates a powerful start to my morning and a strong, reflective end to my day.

Here's a challenge for you:

Get a piece of paper (or your favorite note-taking app).

Make a list of all your negative self-images.

Below that, write an affirmation for each of those negative thoughts.

Next, erase the negative thoughts, leaving only the affirmations.

Make a commitment right now to say these affirmations out loud every morning.

This may seem (or feel) silly, but we promise you, if you approach this with an open mind and make this a part of your daily routine, you will see a change in how you think and feel about yourself. It will have a positive impact on your ability to overcome negativity both from others and from yourself.

Thinking you can be better is one thing, but believing it is everything. This small addition to your daily routine is just one of many ways you can strengthen that belief.

When you are able to really embrace this mindset, you'll find that expecting better of yourself, your colleagues, and your students can build the positive foundation you need to make changes, overcome failures, break through barriers, and Teach Better every day. Yes, it takes work. Yes, you have to constantly push yourself. Yes, you will struggle with this. But through that struggle and hard work will come amazing growth for both you and your students.

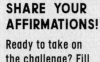

SHARE YOUR AFFIRMATIONS!

Ready to take on the challenge? Fill out the form at teachbetter.com/BookResources to get words of encouragement, inspiration, and support from us over the next year.

> SARAH THOMAS, PhD (@SARAHDATEECHUR)

Regional technology coordinator and founder, EduMatch
sarahjanethomas.com

My last full year in the classroom was chock-full of learning . . . not just for my students but also for me! Having been inspired by my PLN, I changed my philosophy and scrapped "teaching to the test." There were no more test-prep bootcamps or drill-and-kill sessions. Instead, my students learned through inquiry and collaboration with other students around the world.

As a middle school ELA class, of course we wrote; however, this year, we wrote with the intention of connecting with others, of making meaning of the world, and of making change. My students blogged with students in New Zealand, collaborated on persuasive essays with high school students in a different state, and collaborated on a group post to process their thoughts and feelings on social issues.

That year, my students went above and beyond, not just because I expected better of **them**, but mostly because they expected better of **themselves**.

CHAPTER 7
COMPLAIN BETTER

"WHAT YOU'RE SUPPOSED TO DO WHEN YOU DON'T LIKE A THING IS CHANGE IT. IF YOU CAN'T CHANGE IT, CHANGE THE WAY YOU THINK ABOUT IT. DON'T COMPLAIN."

–MAYA ANGELOU

As a new teacher, or even before entering the classroom, we often have visions of grandeur about what our classroom will be and how engaged and excited our students will be within that classroom. In these visions, there is very little that is wrong with education, because we know we can solve all its problems.

In college, most of us think about teaching as a noble, honorable, and exciting profession. We look forward to having our own classes and our own lessons, and negative thoughts very rarely creep into our minds. How many of us have envisioned our students standing on their desks yelling, "Oh captain, my captain!" as we picture ourselves delivering inspiring, life-changing messages?

We play movies in our minds of the ways we would change the lives of even the most challenging students. We will be the support they need when they are struggling, take them under our wings, and proclaim that one inspirational line that will change their lives forever. There is nothing you can say to a passionate preservice teacher that will convince them otherwise!

Rae: *School was a struggle growing up. It seemed that nothing came easily to me. But dance class was the highlight of my week. It was not about the makeup, stage fame, or pretty pink tights and tutus. Honestly, I could have done without the hair spray; rather, it was the culture. Big hugs and excited voices would fill the halls when dance class was about to begin. Every moment, no matter the context, focused on growth and developing into your best self. Regardless of your ability to tendu with a proper turnout, each student in that room celebrated successes together and pushed through failures, knowing the only way forward was to join hands and march together as a team.*

I had the opportunity in my early teen years to teach a dance class, and it was then that I became absolutely, irrevocably hooked on teaching. I knew right then and there that I wanted to take all that I had learned from my experiences teaching dance and build a new type of classroom. One that allowed each student to experience that long-awaited Aha! moment, especially for those students who never believed that moment would come.

Illinois State University's education program did an awesome job to ensure undergraduates had plenty of real-life experience in the classroom. During one of these visits, I remember hearing some of the teachers bemoaning how tired they were and the stress they felt on their shoulders to get students "test ready." They exclaimed these students just weren't getting it and probably wouldn't get it regardless of how many weeks they focused on the topic.

I thought to myself, I will never be like that.

Ah, the blissful naivety of ignorance.

As you well know, the reality of teaching is often far different from the inspirational blockbuster we play in our minds. As we learn more about what the day-to-day challenge of teaching is like, and the realities of the profession begin to smack us in the face, being different becomes easier said than done.

Chad: *Staying positive became more and more difficult every day as I found myself surrounded by negativity, and a piece of advice I received in college became an all-too-real truth.*

While I was working toward my master's degree, a fantastic educator, Sandy Womack, came in to speak. He would later become one of my greatest mentors and my first principal, but something he said that day has stuck with me long after we went our separate ways.

While much of his presentation was inspiring and filled with nuggets of insight, his last piece of advice left me a bit bewildered at the time. As he finished answering various questions from the class, he was asked to provide any final thoughts. He responded with this:

"During your first year, stay out of the teacher's lounge. The only thing that happens there is complaining, and that never helped anyone solve anything."

I was confused.

I remember questioning this statement, based on my earlier and more ignorant ideas about what education was and how all teachers must have the same positive, inspired, and optimistic outlook I did at the time. I mean, it could not possibly be that bad, could it? I wasn't the only teacher who felt the way I did . . . was I? We were all going to change the world together, as a team, right?

———

If your experiences are anything like ours, you quickly found out that Sandy Womack's statement is, unfortunately, accurate. The fact is, teaching is hard. And when something is hard, it is easy to complain about it. More importantly, when something is easy to complain about and you are also surrounded by others who are complaining, the negative mindset is nearly impossible to avoid. It can be incredibly hard to break this complaining habit once you start.

Almost all of us are guilty of becoming what we never thought we would be. We get negative. We get stuck in the whirlwind of "these kids are just never going to get it" and "I can't believe they expect us to implement this new initiative with the lack of training we've had!" You could probably easily add a few hundred other thoughts you've had that don't reflect the kind of teacher you thought you would be.

———

Chad: *I vividly remember sitting with a colleague at lunch one day in the teacher's lounge. We were complaining about how a new initiative our district was implementing was ridiculous, and I was trying to find ways to make it look like I was following suit without actually changing anything. Thinking back, it's both disappointing and amazing. Had we flipped our perspective and focused the time and energy from complaining to figuring out how to actually make it work, we might have been able to positively impact our students.*

I honestly do not remember what the initiative was. What if it was a new idea that could have changed everything for my students? What if it was the key to making my lessons more engaging or my classroom run more smoothly?

Unfortunately, "what if" does not help much. Reflecting on that moment, I realize that I had become the thing that only a short time before I couldn't comprehend being. I had become the teacher about whom Sandy had warned. I had become the reason the teacher's lounge was not a good place for a first-year teacher to spend time.

Whether it was a pointless meeting, a change in state testing, a new initiative, a set of difficult students, or some new obscure rule, expectation, or request that would suck up just a bit more of the time we didn't really have to give, complaining was really easy to do. And, just as Sandy had told us, it never solved anything.

Sure, complaining might have made me feel better for a minute or two, but at the end of the day, the same problems or issues were still there. More importantly, complaining about things never helped us reach more students or improve their learning experiences in our classrooms.

———

As teachers, when we come to this realization, we must make ourselves stop. We must hold ourselves more accountable. We must stop focusing on what or who is to blame for our challenges and instead focus on solutions and on how we can be better for our students.

This is the foundation of everything the Teach Better mindset stands for: solutions, not complaints. Improvement, not excuses.

STOP COMPLAINING. START MAKING CHANGES.

It would be easy to create a long list of all the things that you feel like you have no control over in your classroom, but the reality is that any time something seems out of your control, it is possible to stop, reflect, and find solutions that can help you regain control. At the very least, you'll be able to see the things you can do to better control what happens in your classroom.

- If students are acting out, we can modify our routines, change our entrance or exit procedures, and maybe even rearrange desks.
- If our students are underperforming, we can modify our instruction, differentiate more, or search for some new, more engaging lessons we haven't tried.

- If our administrators don't understand what we are doing in our classroom, we can support our decisions with research, evidence, and explanation.

If you aren't willing to react and change the things you can control, you have no one to blame for the results but yourself. Don't complain; do something. One of Chad's mentors, Amanda Gillespie, always told him, "You may not be able to control everything, but within the four walls of your classroom, you can control almost anything."

If you choose to complain rather than take action to change the problem, you will have succumbed to the system as it is. You will become exactly what you said you wouldn't be. It is only by doing nothing that we accept failure.

––––––––

Tiff: You might say I was a rebellious child. If you were to ask my parents, they would definitely say I was a rebellious child. I never got into any real trouble, and somehow I came through my teenage years relatively unscathed, but I certainly gave my parents their fair share of headaches and stress.

I remember many conversations with my parents, who should be knighted for putting up with me in those challenging years, in which I loudly complained that a certain rule, process, or procedure was not right, would never be right, and was simply not worth following.

My mother, in her seemingly infinite patience and wisdom, said to me:

"Tiffany, there will always be things that are not right. Decisions that are not fair. Rules and laws that make no logical sense. You can choose to follow them, or you can choose to try and change them. If you choose not to try and change them, then you certainly cannot complain about them."

These words stuck with me from that point forward. To this day, they still impact many of the decisions I make. There are endless things in the world of education that are not right, not fair, and not what's best for students. There are endless regulations and dictates and unlimited opportunities to blame things beyond our control, such as administration, government, or parental involvement. The list can go on and on.

When there is something that I just can't live with, something I feel the temptation to complain about, I come back to my mother's words: Change it.

The best place to start the change? In yourself.

––––––––

The charge is simple: Change something! Never settle. Never be okay with things the way they are. You are an amazing, passionate, and talented educator. You have the skills and the knowledge to change the lives of your students.

Great change has never come from complaining.

It comes from action.

ONE MILLION REASONS WHY NOT

Teaching is one of the most difficult professions in the world. Trying to educate students that may be lacking prerequisite skills or are several grade levels behind in their understanding of content is hard. Motivating kids who are unmotivated is not just challenging; it can feel impossible. What we do is hard. Being a teacher is hard. We are overworked, underpaid, and extremely underappreciated.

We all have a million reasons for why that last lesson plan bombed, why Timmy doesn't like our class, or why seventh-grade science is such a tough subject to teach. Let's not forget all those ridiculous management issues you shouldn't have to deal with but do every single day.

Add to that the fact that teachers seem to have less freedom in their classrooms than ever before, not to mention evaluations, state testing, and national and state standards are always looming. And, let's face it, sometimes administrators are not as supportive as they should be. You probably aren't given enough time to plan. You don't feel like you have enough resources to do the job you're being asked to do. And your contract most likely says you should be getting paid for all those extra hours you freely spent at the basketball game.

There are a million reasons why our job is difficult. Because of this, there are a million excuses we could give ourselves for giving up on that botched lesson plan or that difficult student or that new initiative that takes a bit of extra time to embed into our routines. But once we allow these reasons to stop us from giving every ounce of passion we have to impact every student in our classroom, they become excuses. And excuses don't matter. They are useless. They have no place in your classroom.

Even if every excuse we come up with stems from a valid reason or a true challenge we face, we must refuse to accept any of them as a legitimate excuse for not giving everything we have to the calling, the passion, and the mission of education.

It is important at this moment for us to clarify something. We are not telling you to be a martyr; rather, there is a way to strike a balance between giving everything you have to your chosen field and still staying sane and healthy enough to do this amazing, life-changing work. We are also not saying that you shouldn't fight for what's best for the well-being of teachers.

What we are saying is that making excuses is a useless endeavor, and complaining is an absolute waste of your valuable time.

The student sitting in your classroom staring at you every day cannot suffer from your excuses. Your students may not be able to even comprehend the challenges you're facing every day. They have their own problems, their own life challenges, their own worries. They can't take on yours too.

———————

Rae: *Everyone has experienced "that" student, right? The one that fights you tooth and nail on everything. Mine was Valerie.*

"Would you please get out a pencil?"

Valerie wouldn't even think about it.

"Will you try to solve this math problem? I know you can do it!"

Valerie would dish out a record-breaking eye roll.

"Please sit in your assigned seat."

No comment from Valerie here. (Just imagine desks flying.)

It seemed every day was another opportunity for attitude-filled negativity.

My solution? I didn't have one. I had other things going on, and spending time dealing with this nonsense wasn't high on my priority list.

About five months into the school year, I made a phone call home to notify Valerie's family of the horrible behavior occurring in my classroom. (Yes, I did wait this long to begin contacting home.)

There was no answer.

I hunted for an alternative way to contact Valerie's home, but the family only provided one phone number. The next day, I called again.

Still no answer.

I considered that I was calling at a bad time. The next day, I called at a different time of the day.

Again, no answer. My blood was boiling.

I proceeded to call that phone number thirteen more times over the course of a week. On the fourteenth call, an older woman answered. Choking back my frustration, I introduced myself and fought back the urge to explain the irritation I felt not having been able to reach the family. Before even allowing the woman to respond, I began to explain the issues I was seeing in my classroom and the results I predicted if Valerie continued on this path. I blabbered on for almost ten minutes, taking out five months of frustration.

When I finished, I paused for her response, and my heart dropped into the pit of my stomach when I realized she was crying on the other end of the phone. She asked to speak to me in person and wanted to know if she could come to school the following day. We arranged to have a taxi pick her up at home, since she did not have a car.

I felt an onslaught of emotion. Fear, heartbreak, anxiety—you name it, it was in my chest.

The following day I met with Valerie and her grandmother. Struggling to keep from shaking, I shook her grandmother's hand and offered her a seat in my classroom along with Valerie. Then we got right into it.

We spoke for over an hour about the loss of Valerie's mother due to an asthma attack six months prior. We all seemed to fight back tears as Valerie explained she did not know how to tell the school of the loss. Her grandma, now in her late fifties, was taking on four children ranging from second grade to a freshman in high school.

Talk about a reality check.

It's rare that you will fully know and understand someone else's story.

————————

Students care about the attention, effort, and passion you provide them. They might not know it yet, but the impact you have on their educations and their academic successes will stick with them for the rest of their lives. The number of hours you have, the amount of money you're paid, the struggles in your personal life, the resources you aren't given, and the management issues you combat are all simply background noise. In this equation, the only variable that matters is your students and their needs. Of course you care about all those other variables. But your students? These issues are not even on their radar.

When you work with enough educators, you realize that most of the reasons for not trying something and the challenges faced in the classroom are the same no matter where you go, what subject you teach, or what your student population is. Despite the reasons, however, we cannot allow them to be a force strong enough to stop us from doing what is right for our students. They cannot become the thing that prevents us from trying something new, fighting through the stress, overcoming that challenge, and doing anything and everything we can for our students.

We simply cannot accept it. We cannot allow them to stand in our way. You will undoubtedly come across a million reasons why you can't succeed, but they will not stop you. You will not let them. You will rise above them, and you will succeed. Because what you do is simply too important.

What does it take to move past these excuses? To move on from complaining to purposeful action?

Time.

Working to be better requires time. It takes effort. It takes an investment in yourself. If you put in the time and effort to be better (instead of complaining), we promise it will pay off in the best way possible. There is nothing more rewarding than seeing a change you make to your instruction change the way a student looks at education.

The four of us have gotten to a point where almost every excuse is invalid. Not because there isn't merit to the complaint or because it isn't true, but because in the end it simply doesn't matter. Your students matter. Their success matters. Your impact on their life matters.

If you see a fire, do you look for ways to put it out or do you waste time trying to figure out whom to blame for it?

Most of us would agree that you should probably put it out first. The same goes for challenges in your classroom. Stop wasting time looking for someone to blame. Find a solution and make a change. You have a finite amount of time to impact those students, so don't waste it on things that don't matter. Stop worrying about why you can't do something and focus on why you should do it. Instead of focusing on all the things in your way, focus on all the ways you can accomplish the changes you want to see in your classroom.

You are an amazing educator. You have the passion, the skills, and the ability to do amazing things. Your excuses are invalid, but your potential, your knowledge, and your ability to reach more students are absolutely valid, and they are your most powerful assets. Figuring out how to use these skills will always be more important than the reasons you think you can't.

Keep teaching. Keep growing. Keep improving. Your students deserve your best, and so do you.

R.I.S.E. ABOVE THE EXCUSES

You may have been muttering to yourself throughout this chapter thinking that all of this is easy to say and not always easy to do. Let's be honest—none of this is worth anything to you if we don't move on to how you can overcome obstacles, excuses, or fears when they get in your way; in fact, without the next step, this entire chapter is basically as useful as complaining.

When you hit a challenge and you want to complain, you can stop yourself. It is possible! You can make a conscious decision to make a change rather than a complaint. Instead of complaining about a challenge or issue, you can R.I.S.E. above it with these four steps:

1. Reflect on the source of your frustration.
2. Identify potential solutions to the issue.
3. Strategize ways to overcome the challenge.
4. Execute your plan.

If you focus on these four steps, you can flip every challenge, every issue, and every complaint and turn them into solutions. These steps will directly lead you to a more purposeful, productive thought process so you can get back to teaching better.

Let's look at a fairly common problem teachers face on a daily basis and break it down according to the R.I.S.E. model.

SCENARIO

You're frustrated. Your students have been showing up late to your class on a near-daily basis. You find yourself complaining and yelling at your class every day. This makes it difficult to get class started on time. It decreases the time you have to cover the necessary content, and management issues seem to increase in the first ten minutes as kids come in after the bell has already rung.

Because you are frustrated, you start planning for this missed time and even start being more relaxed about the start of class routine. You continue to complain about this to your colleagues, and it starts to affect your attitude and the environment in your classroom. This starts impacting the relationships you have not only with your students but also with your fellow teachers and maybe even your family.

In this scenario, you would be right to be frustrated. Tardiness and delayed start times are common challenges teachers face, so you certainly wouldn't be alone in letting it negatively affect you and your classroom. The problem is that in this scenario, you have accepted this as the norm. You have come to assume that students will be late, and you have modified your start-of-class routine to allow it to continue to happen. Your routine now includes sighs, frustration, and complaining to your colleagues about the issue. Instead of focusing on solving the issue, you've let negativity and circumstances dictate your behavior.

Now, let's look at the same scenario again, but this time you refuse to let the challenge get to you; instead, you focus on how to R.I.S.E. above it and Teach Better. Instead of complaining about the problem and accepting all the excuses for why it is happening, what if you stopped, took a breath, and walked through the steps outlined below? You could turn a negative situation into a powerful moment of reflection that allows you to work toward solving the issue instead of reacting to the consequences of unknown or uncontrolled factors.

The R.I.S.E. process would look something like this:

1. Reflect on the source of your frustration.

Start reflecting by identifying the students who are getting to your class late and all the possible reasons why it happens almost every day. Maybe they're all coming from the same class, and it is on the opposite side of the building. Maybe they're a close-knit group of friends who just get themselves caught up in gossip, slowing them down each day. Maybe there is a lack of respect for the learning that happens in the classroom that needs to be addressed. You should examine all the possible causes.

————

Tiff: *At one point in my career, I was a resource teacher who pulled students out of their classrooms at a set time each week. It was an interesting job that taught me a lot about helping students understand and deal with frustrating content, allowed me to stretch my content understanding to new levels, and gave me the opportunity to collaborate with other teachers frequently.*

One major problem? My schedule depended on teachers sending the students to my room on time. You can probably imagine that this didn't always go smoothly. I often had students coming to my room ten, fifteen, and sometimes thirty minutes late. When you only have fifty minutes with students, those lost minutes become problematic.

There was certainly a lot to complain about in this situation, and I would be lying to you if I said I didn't default to complaining. My husband heard a lot that year about how much a student being ten minutes late could disrupt the best lesson plans. I shared my frustration with some of my colleagues who did my same job at other schools in the district, bemoaned the struggle of getting students to class on time, and expressed how frustrated I was. They all pitched in and shared my frustration. They felt it too!

You are likely not surprised that these venting sessions and shared pity parties did not make me feel better. If anything, they made me angrier!

It all came to a boiling point one week when some of the students arrived at my room forty minutes after class started. Forty minutes! That meant we only had ten minutes left, which was going to be spent exclusively on getting these students integrated into what the rest of the class was doing. I was furious. Livid. It was not a good time to be a student in my class.

I stood up from where I had been working with students, walked to the door and, towering over my little tiny fourth graders, yelled, "You are forty minutes late! At this point, you should have just stayed in your class!"

I felt like those precious ten minutes left in class were useless at that point. There was no way I was going to guide them toward productive learning now. I also felt disrespected, like they had intentionally let me down. I was seeing red with frustration!

Up until that point in the school year, my classroom was well-known among the students I taught as a safe place. It was a place where it was okay to fail, okay to mess up, and okay to just be yourself. The looks on their faces when those angry words escaped my lips told me that I had destroyed what our class was to them. Their silent, open-mouthed stares spoke volumes. One girl looked away to hide the tears coming to her eyes. The slumped-over body language others showed me sent me a clear message.

I had messed up. Badly.

I had betrayed them. I had betrayed myself. I am not a teacher who yells and screams. They had never seen me like that. It felt like I had been punched in the gut, and I was the one who had done it.

I couldn't let that happen. It wasn't fair to my students. It didn't do anything to help solve the problem we were having. And it had undone months—years, even—of the work I'd done building relationships with each one of them.

I had to make a decision. Was I going to continue to complain, letting rage and frustration take over the carefully crafted relationships I had built with my students?

Or was I going to find a solution?

———

Once Tiffany took some time to reflect, she observed that it was always the same students who were late, and that they were always coming from the same teacher. This was the insight she needed to move forward and find solutions. She needed that wake-up call to spur her toward productive reflection and problem-solving.

Reflection is where the process starts, but to solve the problem (so you can stop complaining about it), you must go further.

2. Identify potential solutions to the issue.

Instead of complaining, take the time to discuss the causes of students' tardiness with them, and work with them to identify possible solutions. Maybe your colleague that has them the period before you tends to go past the bell, or maybe they need to stop going to their lockers before your class because simply carrying an additional book with them would solve the issue. Make a list of all possible solutions and include your students in this process. Bringing your students into the conversation will allow them to take more ownership of whatever solution you find together.

––––––

Tiff: When I had a good idea of the problem that contributed to my students' tardiness, I decided to meet with them and problem solve together.

It turned out that their teacher had an incredibly engaging, inspiring, totally awesome morning routine that often went past the school-wide morning meeting scheduled time. The start time for my class was 9:15, the exact time the morning meeting was scheduled to end.

This was clearly a problem for those students caught up in important conversations with their teacher and peers. We had to find a way to make it work, something that would allow those students the time to participate in the awesome morning meeting and still allow them to get to class.

After some brainstorming, students asked whether the start time of my class could be moved back ten minutes.

––––––

Yes! A solution at last. But we all know that moving from an idea to successful implementation of that idea is not always easy. Time for more brainstorming!

3. Strategize ways to overcome the challenge.

Now that you have an idea (or multiple ideas) of how to solve the problem, it is time to focus on how you can implement those potential solutions. Again, bring students into this process. Involving them in turning an idea into reality not only helps you solve the problem but also helps them understand what real-world problem-solving looks like. You may also need to have conversations with your colleagues or even your administration to lay out a plan for tackling the issue at hand.

Tiff: Moving the start time for my class backward ten minutes was a great idea, but I couldn't do it alone. My schedule was complex that year; I was teaching ten classes in two different schools while collaborating with eighteen teachers, and it was a tad bit tricky. I told my students it wouldn't happen quickly and would involve many conversations, but that we now had a plan to try and solve their problem (and mine).

So now I had to put in the work. I made phone calls, sent emails, made more phone calls, and held several in-person meetings before I finally received the approval I needed to move the class time.

It certainly took some work. I spent quite a bit of time on these conversations. I even got some pushback from teachers who were happy with the schedule the way it was originally. But I was excited to be on my way to finding and implementing a solution.

Reflection? Check! Identifying solutions? Check! Strategizing? Check! But it can all fall apart without the last step.

4. Execute your plan.

Once you have that plan, it's time to enforce it. Stay focused, stay firm. If you've properly completed steps one through three, you should be able to overcome the challenge. And if the plan does not work after you've made your best efforts, it might be time to go back to step one and rework the process to find a better solution.

Tiff: The ten-minute change of our class start time resolved many of the issues we'd been facing. In the first few weeks of the plan, I rarely had a student late to class.

Of course, as with many things in teaching, it needed modification and upkeep to stay effective. You know the teacher with the awesome morning meetings? She still forgot to send kids to me sometimes. It happened less often, but it still happened.

So I modified! I would send out weekly tidbits to teachers with an instructional idea they could use in their classrooms. This would always come out the day before I was supposed to see their students, and at the end of the email, I would add a quick message saying how much I was looking forward to seeing students A, B, and C in class the next day. This gentle reminder did the trick almost every time. If student tardiness worsened, I would make sure to have lunch with the teacher and chat about the students. Keeping myself in the forefront of the teacher's mind helped the situation immensely.

I also made a point to regularly thank teachers for being willing to adjust the class time.

The bottom line was that I set the routine, made adjustments as needed, and maintained consistent communication to ensure that the solution my students and I found together would be successful.

The most important part of this whole process is to remove the belief that some problems are unsolvable. It is time to believe that you can rise above them. By working through the four R.I.S.E. steps, it is possible to identify a solution and implement a plan to fix the problem.

AN END AND A BEGINNING

Here we are, nearing the end of our journey together through this book.

Teaching is hard. It is an impossible job with unrealistic expectations and problems beyond what we ever could have imagined as education majors in college. You have walked through the chapters of this book, exploring the dozens of ways you can work to Teach Better for your students, always striving to be better than you were before.

Now, in these final words, all four of us challenge you to transform your complaints into action. Right now, identify something you can transform in your classroom. Identify a complaint on which you are willing to take action. Identify a place where you can grow together with your students, your colleagues, and your administration.

Break out a notebook or record a voice memo and choose. Note what you are most prone to complain about. Begin the steps of the R.I.S.E. process. If you can't begin right now, get your phone (we know it can't be too far from where you are), and set an appointment in your calendar for when you will begin.

We can only Teach Better when we are willing to take action. Relentlessly pursue the impact you envisioned when you started your teaching journey. Do it with passion, drive, commitment, and hope.

Wherever you start, wherever you go in your journey to Teach Better, remember that it is always possible. It is possible to strive for more. It is possible to achieve your dreams as a teacher. It is possible to reach the unreachable student.

It is possible to be better.

ACKNOWLEDGMENTS
FROM THE TEAM

Thank yous go out to . . .

- Dave and Shelley Burgess for taking a chance on four new authors.
- Heather Koehl for believing in us before we even believed in ourselves.
- Matt White for instilling the "Stop Selling, Start Helping" mindset in everything we do.
- Keith Minton for seeing our vision and helping us get there.
- The teachers, schools, and districts who believe in and implement our message, mission, and vision for education.
- Rick Stockburger and Courtney Gras for helping guide our vision in the very early stages of this new adventure.

Chad Ostrowski: I Acknowledge . . .

- My Wife Amelia and Children: Dylan, Autumn, Emily, and Alex for their sacrifices and unwavering support of my dreams and vision for education.

- My mother, Barb Schollaert, for inspiring me as an educator and supporting me in everything I do, and My father, Richard Ostrowski, and stepfather, David Schollaert, for their guidance, belief, and dedication to my success.
- My mentors, principals, and colleagues who have helped me learn, grow, and thrive as an educator.
- The Teach Better Team (Jeff, Rae, and Tiffany) for helping make all of this a reality.
- Jeff Gargas, for listening to a story about a teacher he knew and wanting to do more than "just make an e-book."

Jeff Gargas: I Acknowledge . . .

- My wife, Amy, the reason I do anything I do.
- My kids, Jonathan and Jacquelyn, who keep me on my toes and remind me that life is meant to be a continuous stream of laughter sprinkled with hugs and kisses.
- Mom and Dad Gargas, for making sure, no matter what, I knew I could do whatever I set my mind to.
- Yummie and Yuckie for trusting that one of my crazy ideas will work out one day.
- My brothers, Mark and Paul, for supporting me no matter what, and always keeping me grounded.
- Chad Ostrowski, for coming up with a silly idea about education, and trusting me to help share it with the world.

Rae Hughart: I Acknowledge . . .

- My husband, Daniel Hughart, for the continued support of making twenty-hour workdays feel like a breeze!
- My incredibly generous parents, Jim and Julie Ford, for their relentless focus on working toward your passion and taking each moment as an opportunity for a connection.
- My awe-inspiring sister, Dana Ford, for our continued battle to be the favorite in the family. Resting has never been an option against you— you are tough competition!

- My grandma, Sima Browne, for never allowing my learning disability to limit my success. Thank you for the years of after-school tutoring sessions and inspiration which finally allowed me to achieve my dreams of going to college!
- To the friends whom we always treated like family, Anne and Jeff Levin, Mary and Cary Johnson, Rabbi Paul, and Cathy Cohen, thank you for acting as wonderful role models throughout my upbringing.
- And let's break the rules and acknowledge my two adorable puppies, Mr. Harvey Dent and Mr. Alfred Pennyworth, for more dog snuggles and love a girl could ask for!

Tiffany Ott: I Acknowledge . . .

- My husband, Cameron, for sending me out the door at 6 a.m. for months on end to go write in a coffee shop while he took care of everything else in our lives.
- My three amazing, crazy, exhausting, and inspiring children for making me a better human every single day.
- Jeff Gargas for turning a playdate for our kids at the park into a life-changing opportunity.
- My parents, for helping me believe that my childhood dream of changing the world wasn't just a fantasy.
- My sister, Jessica Orlovsky, for letting me tag along to her classroom one day—and changing my life forever.

MORE FROM

Since 2012, DBCI has been publishing books that inspire and equip educators to be their best. For more information on our DBCI titles or to purchase bulk orders for your school, district, or book study, visit DaveBurgessconsulting. com/DBCIbooks.

MORE FROM THE *LIKE A PIRATE*™ SERIES

- *Teach Like a PIRATE* by Dave Burgess
- *eXPlore Like a Pirate* by Michael Matera
- *Learn Like a Pirate* by Paul Solarz
- *Play Like a Pirate* by Quinn Rollins
- *Run Like a Pirate* by Adam Welcome

LEAD *LIKE A PIRATE*™ SERIES

- *Lead Like a PIRATE* by Shelley Burgess and Beth Houf
- *Balance Like a Pirate* by Jessica Cabeen, Jessica Johnson, and Sarah Johnson
- *Lead beyond Your Title* by Nili Bartley
- *Lead with Culture* by Jay Billy
- *Lead with Literacy* by Mandy Ellis

LEADERSHIP & SCHOOL CULTURE

- *Culturize* by Jimmy Casas
- *Escaping the School Leader's Dunk Tank* by Rebecca Coda and Rick Jetter
- *From Teacher to Leader* by Starr Sackstein

- *The Innovator's Mindset* by George Couros
- *Kids Deserve It!* by Todd Nesloney and Adam Welcome
- *Let Them Speak* by Rebecca Coda and Rick Jetter
- *The Limitless School* by Abe Hege and Adam Dovico
- *The Pepper Effect* by Sean Gaillard
- *The Principled Principal* by Jeffrey Zoul and Anthony McConnell
- *Relentless* by Hamish Brewer
- *The Secret Solution* by Todd Whitaker, Sam Miller, and Ryan Donlan
- *Start. Right. Now.* by Todd Whitaker, Jeffrey Zoul, and Jimmy Casas
- *Stop. Right. Now.* by Jimmy Casas and Jeffrey Zoul
- *They Call Me "Mr. De"* by Frank DeAngelis
- *Unmapped Potential* by Julie Hasson and Missy Lennard
- *Word Shift* by Joy Kirr
- *Your School Rocks* by Ryan McLane and Eric Lowe

TECHNOLOGY & TOOLS

- *50 Things You Can Do with Google Classroom* by Alice Keeler and Libbi Miller
- *50 Things to Go Further with Google Classroom* by Alice Keeler and Libbi Miller
- *140 Twitter Tips for Educators* by Brad Currie, Billy Krakower, and Scott Rocco
- *Block Breaker* by Brian Aspinall
- *Code Breaker* by Brian Aspinall
- *Google Apps for Littles* by Christine Pinto and Alice Keeler
- *Master the Media* by Julie Smith
- *Shake Up Learning* by Kasey Bell
- *Social LEADia* by Jennifer Casa-Todd
- *Teaching Math with Google Apps* by Alice Keeler and Diana Herrington
- *Teachingland* by Amanda Fox and Mary Ellen Weeks

TEACHING METHODS & MATERIALS

- *All 4s and 5s* by Andrew Sharos
- *The Classroom Chef* by John Stevens and Matt Vaudrey
- *Ditch That Homework* by Matt Miller and Alice Keeler
- *Ditch That Textbook* by Matt Miller
- *Don't Ditch That Tech* by Matt Miller, Nate Ridgway, and Angelia Ridgway
- *EDrenaline Rush* by John Meehan
- *Educated by Design* by Michael Cohen, The Tech Rabbi
- *The EduProtocol Field Guide* by Marlena Hebern and Jon Corippo
- *The EduProtocol Field Guide: Book 2* by Marlena Hebern and Jon Corippo
- *Instant Relevance* by Denis Sheeran
- *LAUNCH* by John Spencer and A.J. Juliani
- *Make Learning MAGICAL* by Tisha Richmond
- *Pure Genius* by Don Wettrick
- *The Revolution* by Darren Ellwein and Derek McCoy
- *Shift This!* by Joy Kirr
- *Spark Learning* by Ramsey Musallam
- *Sparks in the Dark* by Travis Crowder and Todd Nesloney
- *Table Talk Math* by John Stevens
- *The Wild Card* by Hope and Wade King
- *The Writing on the Classroom Wall* by Steve Wyborney

INSPIRATION, PROFESSIONAL GROWTH & PERSONAL DEVELOPMENT

- *Be REAL* by Tara Martin
- *Be the One for Kids* by Ryan Sheehy
- *Creatively Productive* by Lisa Johnson
- *The EduNinja Mindset* by Jennifer Burdis
- *Empower Our Girls* by Lynmara Colón and Adam Welcome

- *The Four O'Clock Faculty* by Rich Czyz
- *How Much Water Do We Have?* by Pete and Kris Nunweiler
- *P Is for Pirate* by Dave and Shelley Burgess
- *A Passion for Kindness* by Tamara Letter
- *The Path to Serendipity* by Allyson Apsey
- *Sanctuaries* by Dan Tricarico
- *Shattering the Perfect Teacher Myth* by Aaron Hogan
- *Stories from Webb* by Todd Nesloney
- *Talk to Me* by Kim Bearden
- *Teach Me, Teacher* by Jacob Chastain
- *TeamMakers* by Laura Robb and Evan Robb
- *Through the Lens of Serendipity* by Allyson Apsey
- *The Zen Teacher* by Dan Tricarico

CHILDREN'S BOOKS

- *Beyond Us* by Aaron Polansky
- *Cannonball In* by Tara Martin
- *Dolphins in Trees* by Aaron Polansky
- *I Want to Be a Lot* by Ashley Savage
- *The Princes of Serendip* by Allyson Apsey
- *Zom-Be a Design Thinker* by Amanda Fox

BRING THE TEACH BETTER MESSAGE TO YOUR SCHOOL OR DISTRICT EVENT

www.teachbetter.com

All speakers can present on the Teach Better mindset, and customized presentations are available upon request.

CHAD OSTROWSKI

Chad is the cofounder of the Teach Better Team and the creator of The Grid Method, but he is a middle school science teacher at heart. He now travels the country sharing his story, working with teachers, schools, and districts to help them reach more students.

TOPICS

- Increasing Student Achievement
- Staff Motivation
- The Power of Mastery Learning
- Transforming Your Instruction
- The Teach Better mindset
- Grading and Assessment
- Classroom Management
- Differentiation / Meeting Student Needs
- Initiative Rollout and Implementation

PRESENTATIONS / KEYNOTES
Reaching ALL Students with Mastery Learning

Participants will learn the following:

- Tools and strategies to effectively implement mastery learning
- How to increase student ownership and achievement
- How to transform your classroom

Teach Better.

Participants will learn the following:

- Where Teach Better came from
- How to apply the Teach Better mindset to your practice
- The positive impacts of the Teach Better mindset on practice, instruction and success

7 Changes That Could Save Your Teaching Career

Participants will learn the following:

- High impact teaching strategies
- How to change your mindset to overcome challenges in the classroom
- How to reignite your passion for teaching

TIFFANY OTT

Tiffany Ott is the director of curriculum development with the Teach Better Team and a high school math teacher in Ohio. Tiffany is also the founder of #MasteryChat and an educational technology fanatic.

As a ten-year veteran classroom teacher, she discovered a passion for meaningful technology integration. Now she combines her love of great ed tech with a mastery learning approach to teaching and learning, transforming her class, her teaching, and her students' learning, and sharing her strategies with educators around the country.

TOPICS

- Educational Technology
- Gifted Education

- Staff Inspiration
- The Power of Mastery Learning
- The Teach Better mindset

PRESENTATIONS / KEYNOTES
Reaching Gifted Students in ALL Service Settings with Mastery Learning

Participants will learn the following:

- Tools and strategies to effectively implement mastery learning
- How to increase student ownership and achievement
- How to transform your classroom

Making Mastery Manageable with Effective Technology Integration

Participants will learn the following:

- How today's technology makes mastery learning possible
- Technology tools and resources to enhance instruction in your classroom
- How to transform the way your students think about their education

Bite-Size Mastery: Nibbling Your Way through Mastery Learning

Participants will learn the following:

- The foundations of mastery learning—and why it doesn't have to be scary!
- The common pitfalls of mastery learning
- How to break down and align your standards
- How to design high quality, engaging, and effective initial instruction
- Timing instruction, assessment, and learning opportunities for maximum effectiveness
- Planning for and organizing the learning process in a bite-sized mastery lesson

RAE HUGHART

Rae Hughart is a middle-level math educator in Illinois, creator of the Teach Further Model, and the director of training and development for the Teach Better Team. In 2017, Rae was honored with the Illinois State University Outstanding Young Alumni Award, inducting her into the University Hall of Fame.

TOPICS

- Dynamic Lesson Planning
- Student Motivation
- Staff Inspiration
- Community Engagement
- The Power of Mastery Learning
- Standards-Based Grading (SBG)
- Growth Mindset / Mindfulness
- The Teach Better mindset

PRESENTATIONS / KEYNOTES
Your Mindset Leads to Your Impact

Participants will learn the following:

- The connection between personal growth and its ability to stifle our educational growth
- Tools on a mindfulness practice of goal setting
- How your network can transform your impact
- How to actively choosing to excel

PBL + Maker + STEM + Community = Purpose! #TeachFurther

Participants will learn the following:

- The three pillars of dynamic, community inspired lessons
- How to enhance any lesson for any subject area at any grade level
- Why you should teach beyond the four walls of your classroom

Diving in Head First into Standards-Based Grading

Participants will learn the following:

- The fundamental four pillars of standards-based grading
- How to combat common concerns
- What scores represent in sbg
- Manageable retake strategies
- How standards-based grading can transform the way you teach

Mastering Personalized Learning in the Twenty-First Century

Participants will learn the following:

- Tools and strategies to effectively reach more students
- How to increase student ownership and accountability
- How to integrate current tools with purpose

JEFF GARGAS

Jeff is the COO and cofounder of the Teach Better Team. Prior to Teach Better, Jeff spent most of his career in the hospitality and entertainment industries. In the five years prior to cofounding Teach Better, he worked with small businesses and entrepreneurs, helping them with content marketing, brand management, social media, and general business operations.

TOPICS

- Entrepreneurship / Teacherpreneurship
- Initiative Implementation
- Social Media
- Leadership
- The Teach Better mindset

PRESENTATIONS / KEYNOTES
Increasing Your Impact through Entrepreneurship

Participants will learn the following:

- The increased impact teacherpreneurs can have on education
- How to find your niche
- How to share your passion with other educators

Using Social Media to Engage Your Students and Community

Participants will learn the following:

- How to effectively engage students using social media
- How to keep yourself and your students safe on social media
- How to engage stakeholders using social media

#Do It Anyway—How to Overcome Fear, Negativity, and Criticism and Do What's Right for You

Participants will learn the following:

- How to embrace failure to grow
- How to convert negativity and criticism into passion and creativity
- Why what others think should not stop you from pursuing your dreams
- How to feel the fear of failure—and do it anyway

Classroom Inc: How to Manage Your Classroom like a Business and Your Business like A Classroom

Participants will learn the following:

- The similarities between classrooms and businesses
- Why teachers and business leaders have more in common than they think
- Strategies for effectively working with others, managing teams (Or classrooms!), and building lifelong, impactful relationships

Made in the USA
Middletown, DE
28 September 2019